SELECTED POEMS

LOUIS MACNEICE

Selected Poems

Edited by
MICHAEL LONGLEY

faber and faber

First published in 1988
by Faber and Faber Limited
Bloomsbury House
77–74 Great Russell Street
London WC1B 3DA
This new paperback edition first published in 2007

Photoset by RefineCatch Limited, Bungay, Suffolk
Printed in England by TJ International Ltd, Padstow, Cornwall

A CIP record for this book
is available from the British Library

ISBN 978-0-571-23381-6
ISBN 0-571-23381-3

FSC
www.fsc.org
MIX
Paper from
responsible sources
FSC® C013056

Thalassa

Run out the boat, my broken comrades;
Let the old seaweed crack, the surge
Burgeon oblivious of the last
Embarkation of feckless men,
Let every adverse force converge –
Here we must needs embark again.

Run up the sail, my heartsick comrades;
Let each horizon tilt and lurch –
You know the worst: your wills are fickle,
Your values blurred, your hearts impure
And your past life a ruined church –
But let your poison be your cure.

Put out to sea, ignoble comrades,
Whose record shall be noble yet;
Butting through scarps of moving marble
The narwhal dares us to be free;
By a high star our course is set,
Our end is Life. Put out to sea.

Contents

Preface

The text printed here follows the latest reprint (1987) of the *Collected Poems* which was edited by E. R. Dodds and first published in 1966.

I have arranged the poems according to their appearance in individual volumes. The earlier poems, therefore, are not always in the sequence adopted by MacNeice in the *Collected Poems* of 1949 and modified by Dodds. This affects the placing of the eclogues, 'Valediction', 'The Hebrides', 'Trilogy for X', 'The Casualty' and 'Western Landscape'.

Dodds provides dates for most of the poems and includes them in the text as well as in the contents pages. With the exception of 'The Closing Album', the only work dated by MacNeice in the *Collected Poems* of 1949, I have confined dates of composition to the contents pages.

'Thalassa', the last poem in the *Collected Poems*, I have used here as an epigraph. There is some doubt as to its date of composition, and it makes in any case as fit an epigraph as a finale. This selection ends with 'Coda', the last poem in *The Burning Perch*.

I am grateful to Oxford University Press for permission to include examples of MacNeice's prose from *Modern Poetry* and the *Selected Literary Criticism of Louis MacNeice*.

M.L.

Introduction

Louis MacNeice revisited and revised his past throughout his career, and he believed that 'a certain knowledge of the poet's personal background will help us to understand him, for his language is to some extent personal'. He was born 'in Belfast between the mountain and the gantries' in 1907. His parents came originally from the West of Ireland. In 1909 the family moved to Carrickfergus on the County Antrim side of Belfast Lough where his father, later a bishop, had been appointed Church of Ireland (Anglican) rector. MacNeice admired his father and, although he rejected orthodoxy, kept his mind open to religious possibility: 'a tall tree sprouted from his father's grave.' The illness, mental breakdown and early death of his mother disturbed MacNeice for the rest of his life:

> When I was five the black dreams came;
> Nothing after was quite the same.

He was educated in England at Sherborne preparatory school, Marlborough, and Merton College, Oxford: 'Schooled from the age of ten to a foreign voice.' His first marriage, to Mary Ezra, took place in 1930. They had one son, Daniel. During the 1930s he lectured in classics at Birmingham University and Bedford College, London: 'As impresario of the Ancient Greeks.' Up to a point he shared the political and aesthetic concerns of the English 'thirties poets', although he criticized their appetite for ideology. In 1936 he visited Iceland with W. H. Auden, and they collaborated on *Letters from Iceland*. He spent most of 1940 in America but returned to England by December because 'I thought I was missing History'. ('Brother Fire' draws on his experiences as a fire warden in the London Blitz.) He married Hedli Anderson, the actress and singer, in the summer of 1942. Their daughter Corinna was born a year later. In 1941 he joined the BBC. Until 1961, when he turned freelance, MacNeice wrote and produced programmes for the Features Department, a creative powerhouse of the time. MacNeice's poetic parable-play *The Dark Tower* is his most celebrated radio work. Besides publishing twelve collections of poems he translated Aeschylus and Goethe; wrote criticism, journalism and autobiography. Anyone who responds to MacNeice's poetry should read *The Strings are False*, an autobiographical distillation up to 1941. His critical books (*Modern Poetry*, *The Poetry of W. B. Yeats*, *Varieties of Parable*, recently augmented by the *Selected Literary Criticism of Louis MacNeice*) complement the poetry in another way. His lucid and passionate criticism is central to our understanding of twentieth-century poetry. The circumstances of MacNeice's death oddly and sadly reflect his commitment to art and to his own images. He died of pneumonia in 1963 after descending into Yorkshire pot-holes with BBC sound engineers who were recording effects for his last radio play, *Persons from Porlock*.

In 'Carrick Revisited' MacNeice exclaims: 'Time and place – our bridgeheads into reality / But also its concealment!' Thus, if poetry is conditioned by life, it is also a quest to interpret this conditioning. Three conjunctions of time and place particularly obsessed Mac-Neice's imagination: the North of Ireland; the West of Ireland; Birmingham and London as the joint context of 'an evil time' for Britain and Europe. He terms the West of Ireland 'the first of [my] dream worlds'. The North was the first of his nightmare worlds. *The Strings are False* tells us a lot about his childhood responses to that complex scene, its blend of the frightening and the picturesque. The extremes of Northern Irish life touched him early – the bloody banging of Lambeg drums, the squalor in which the Carrickfergus Catholics lived:

> The Scotch Quarter was a line of residential houses
> But the Irish Quarter was a slum for the blind and halt.

Ulster became for MacNeice a place hard with basalt and iron, cacophonous with 'Fog-horn, mill-horn, corncrake and church bell', 'the hooting of lost sirens and the clang of trams', 'the voodoo of the Orange bands'. Narrow religion and life-denying puritanism mark the point at which socio-political 'darkest Ulster' merges into the more personal aspects of MacNeice's childhood. When he was still very young he was looked after by a woman who embodied the least desirable Northern Irish qualities. 'Her face was sour and die-hard Puritanical . . . she knew all there was to be known about bringing up children; keep them conscious of sin, learn them their sums, keep all the windows shut tight.' He was afraid of his father's 'conspiracy with God':

> My father made the walls resound,
> He wore his collar the wrong way round.

He was terrorized by nightmares, by the shadows in the rectory (actual and psychological), by a precocious sense of sin and guilt which is still vivid in 'The Blasphemies'. His mother's inexplicable withdrawal was the central element of this Ulster cosmos:

In the beginning was the Irish rain . . . I pressed my nose against the streaming nursery window for a glimpse of the funeral procession on its way to the cemetery the other side of the hawthorn hedge. Our life was bounded by this hedge; a granite obelisk would look over it here, and there across the field of corncrakes could be seen a Norman castle, and trains would pass as if to the ends of Ireland . . . but, by and narrow, our damp cramped acre was our world. The human elements of this world need not be detailed: guilt, hell fire, Good Friday, the doctor's cough, hurried lamps in the night, melancholia, mongolism, violent sectarian voices. All this sadness and conflict and attrition and frustration were set in this one acre near the smoky town within sound not only of the tolling bell, but of the smithy that seemed to defy it.

On Good Fridays he would 'walk up and down the garden, keeping my face austere, trying not to be pleased by the daffodils'. Fantasy, make-believe and above all a relish for the sensory world were the antidotes he evolved to vanquish religion, darkness, loneliness, fears of death and petrifaction. These childhood antidotes anticipated in miniature the strategies of the adult poet. MacNeice's many words for light, and images of light, remember his Ulster darkness: glitter, rainbow, dazzle, glint, 'a sliver of peacock light', 'sunlight on the garden', 'timeless prism'. In particular, all the relationships of light to water shape his concept of flux. 'The dazzle on the sea' defies the 'stalactites and stalagmites' of his upbringing.

The West glimmered in family conversation and at the back of his mind. 'The very name Connemara seemed too rich for any ordinary place. It appeared to be a country of windswept open spaces and mountains blazing with whins and seas that were never quiet . . . But I was not to visit Achill or Connemara until I had left school. So for many years I lived on a nostalgia for somewhere I had never been.' Nostalgia, the ache for the voyage home, intensified when he got to know the landscape. In 'The Strand' he remembers walking beside the sea with his father, 'A square black figure whom the horizon understood.' At first this suggests someone who belongs, unlike his displaced son, in such transitory terrain:

> But then as now the floor mop of the foam
> Blotted the bright reflections – and no sign
>
> Remains of face or feet when visitors have gone home.

Tom Paulin has responded sensitively to the poem: 'A strand is never quite a place, a really rooted locus, and that word "visitors" is filled with a sense of dispossession – it is the word used in the West of Ireland to describe tourists.' This is true, but the sense of imperma-nence is further heightened if death is read as the watermark behind the last isolated line. Everyone everywhere is a tourist – not just Louis MacNeice. Derek Mahon has repudiated the notion that MacNeice's residence in England puts his 'Irishness' in doubt: ' "A tourist in his own country", it has been said, with the implication that this is somehow discreditable. But of what sensitive person is the same not true? The phrase might stand, indeed, as an epitaph for Modern Man, beside Camus's "He made love and read the news-papers".' In 'Western Landscape', MacNeice's sense of being a holiday visitor modulates into a larger cultural and religious medi-tation. He terms himself 'a bastard / Out of the West by urban civilization': he feels 'disfranchised / In the constituencies of quartz and bog-oak', neither 'Free of all roots nor yet a rooted peasant'. But, at a deeper level, this remarkable poem, or more particularly its central stretch from lines 19 to 75, demonstrates at its most intrepid MacNeice's spiritual quest:

> O relevance of cloud and rock –
> If such could be our permanence!

Desperate yet joyous, 'improvised', the poem throws in obdurate details like wrack and screes and sheep among swooning adverbs and apostrophes, the verse itself tumbling down the page from one lucky rhyme to the next, to create a transcendental moment bodied forth by the five senses, a hymn to the 'quintessential West' as the poet's last resort.

In *The Poetry of W. B. Yeats* MacNeice compares Yeats to Lancelot 'who nearly saw the Grael':

He believed in the Grael, *divining* its presence . . . he made great efforts to achieve direct vision. But it was perhaps just because he lacked this direct vision that he was able to write poetry. Would not Lancelot have been able to give a better account of the Quest than Galahad? Galahad, I feel, would have forgotten the road in the goal achieved and have lost his human feelings in that superhuman experience.

If one part of MacNeice's imagination is metaphysical, the other insists that 'the poet's first business is *mentioning* things'. This was especially his priority in the 1930s when the social and political situation made 'subject matter' seem paramount: 'Poets today are working back from luxury-writing and trying once more to become functional.' However, MacNeice's poetry was never put at the service of political opinions or revolutionary scenarios as was that of Stephen Spender and Cecil Day Lewis. He prefaces *Modern Poetry* with a considered testament:

> The poet is a maker, not a retail trader. The writer today should be not so much the mouthpiece of a community (for then he will only tell it what it knows already) as its conscience, its critical faculty, its generous instinct. In a world intransigent and overspecialized, falsified by practical necessities, the poet must maintain his elasticity and refuse to tell lies to order. Others can tell lies more efficiently; no one except the poet can give us poetic truth.

MacNeice brought to bear on English society his Irish conditioning and perspectives. In 'Eclogue from Iceland' he speaks in the persona of Ryan:

> My diehard countrymen like drayhorses
> Drag their ruin behind them.
> Shooting straight in the cause of crooked thinking
> Their greed is sugared with pretence of public spirit.
> From all which I am an exile.

Ireland inoculated MacNeice against political certainties and false optimism. He was less likely than most to succumb to 'the pitiless abstractions'. But, as he was later to assert, 'to shun dogma does not mean to renounce belief'. The rise of fascism and the Spanish Civil War demanded a moral stance:

> Minute your gesture but it must be made –
> Your hazard, your act of defiance and hymn of hate,
> Hatred of hatred, assertion of human values,
> Which is now your only duty.

One of MacNeice's strategies was to report, to bear witness. He packed the contemporary world into his poetry: 'A turning page of shine and sound, the day's maze.' Like most true poets he relished making catalogues, whether of place names ('West Meon, Tisted, Farnham, Woking, Weybridge') or film-stars ('Cagney, Lombard, Bing and Garbo') or things ('Cubical scent-bottles artificial legs arctic foxes and electric mops'). Seldom can the lyric have carried so much freight and remained airborne. In 'Snow', probably his most famous poem, 'World is crazier and more of it than we think, / Incorrigibly plural'. The motto most readers would attach to MacNeice's *œuvre* is, unavoidably, 'The drunkenness of things being various'. Philip Larkin followed this line in his *New Statesman* obituary:

> When we were young . . . his poetry was the poetry of our everyday life, of shop-windows, traffic policemen, ice-cream soda, lawn-mowers, and an uneasy awareness of what the newsboys were shouting. In addition he displayed a sophisticated sentimentality about falling leaves and lipsticked cigarette stubs: he could have written the words of 'These Foolish Things'. We were grateful to him for having found a place in poetry for these properties . . .

Autumn Journal is the apotheosis of MacNeice's desire to fit everything in. Written from August to December 1938 at the time of the Munich crisis, this long work intertwines public event and private concern, allowing one to illuminate the other. As the poem's interrogating 'spotlight' roves from present to past and back again, there are sections about MacNeice's life at school and university, a current love affair, Spain, Ireland, Birmingham, the world of Ancient Greece. In a letter to T. S. Eliot, MacNeice explains the division into sections which gives *Autumn Journal* its '*dramatic* quality, as different parts of myself (e.g. the anarchist, the defeatist, the sensual man, the philosopher, the would-be good citizen) can be given their say in turn.' He goes on: 'It contains reportage, metaphysics, ethics, lyrical emotion, autobiography, nightmare. There is constant interrelation of abstract and concrete. Generalizations balanced by pictures . . . it is both a panorama and a confession of faith.' Somehow everything comes together poetically in MacNeice's courageous summoning of all available human resources against anarchy and despair. *Autumn Journal* is the opposite of Art for Art's Sake: yet, paradoxically, as he accepts the challenge of variety, impurity, vulgarity – all terms of praise in his critical lexicon – MacNeice's lyricism intensifies. The author of this 'autumnal palinode' more than answers his own celebrated job description:

> I would have a poet able-bodied, fond of talking, a reader of the newspapers, capable of pity and laughter, informed in economics, appreciative of women, involved in personal relationships, actively interested in politics, susceptible to physical impressions.

The poet as all-rounder is also manifest in MacNeice's vocabulary and imagery. Many argots enrich the cornucopian flow of *Autumn Journal* – for instance, those of philosophy, politics, classical and popular culture. Slangy vitality and rhetorical resonance merge in the poem's 'intercrossing / Coloured waters':

> Sun shines easy but I no longer
> Docket a place in the sun –
> No wife, no ivory tower, no funk-hole.
> The night grows purple, the crisis hangs
> Over the roofs like a Persian army
> And all of Xenophon's parasangs
> Would take us only an inch from danger.
> Black-out practice and A.R.P.,
> Newsboys driving a roaring business,
> The flapping paper snatched to see
> If anything has, or has not, happened.
> And I go to the Birmingham Hippodrome
> Packed to the roof and primed for laughter
> And beautifully at home
> With the ukulele and the comic chestnuts;
> 'As pals we meet, as pals we part' –
> Embonpoint and a new tiara;
> The comedian spilling the apple-cart
> Of *double entendres* and doggerel verses.

MacNeice was as interested as the comedian in *double entendres*. He believed that 'the poet is a specialist in something which everyone practises', that spoken idiom, especially urban demotic, is an imaginative resource. His later poetry not only relishes idioms and clichés but probes their hidden codes. 'The Slow Starter' broods on a proverb; 'Round the Corner' opens out the implications of an everyday phrase; in 'The Taxis' the trade term 'extra' and the jingle 'tra-la' become increasingly sinister. MacNeice gets inside words. His imagery, too, combines variety of content with variety of treatment. In his brilliant essay, 'Experiences with Images', written in 1949 during a period of slow creative transition, he suggests:

> Of the endless complexities of imagery an astonishing number are exemplified in Shakespeare. Most poets are far more narrowly conditioned; thus few can take both their reading and their physical sensations in their stride and few are equally at ease with

the image that pinpoints in and with the image that ripples out. Shakespeare seems at home with all sorts – with description and incantation, with the cerebral and the sensuous, with the functional and the decorative, with the topical and the time-honoured, with the nonsense hyperbole and the algebraic cipher, with the grass that is green and the red that is rhetoric, with learned allusion and first-hand observation, with straight punch and hook, with one-word nuance and embroidered conceit.

In applauding Shakespeare's 'catholic receptivity' MacNeice reveals his own ambition.

The pressure of childhood experience seems to have set up chain reactions of imagery throughout his poetry. The dark side of his mind generates images of 'fear, anxiety, loneliness or monotony', of mortality, stasis and the iron forces controlling human affairs: bells as 'skulls' mouths'; 'Great black birds that fly alone / Slowly through a land of stone'; 'every evil iron / Siren'; 'visitors in masks or in black glasses'; 'the accusing clock'; 'the dog-dark hall'; 'The gigantic scales in the sky'. If we compare the early poem 'River in Spate' with the late poem 'Charon', we can see, as MacNeice did in a commentary on *The Burning Perch*, 'both the continuity and the difference'. 'River in Spate' was originally called 'A Cataract Conceived as the March of Corpses'. MacNeice imagines the sound of gushing water as a succession of 'cold funerals' grotesquely speeded up:

> And helter-skelter the coffins come and the drums beat and
>   the waters flow,
> And the panther horses lift their hooves and paw and shift and
>   draw the bier,
> The corpses blink in the rush of the river, and out of the water
>   their chins they tip
> And quaff the gush and lip the draught and crook their heads
>   and crow . . .

The poem comes 'helter-skelter' too: the ever-unravelling syntax of its single sentence, the cascade of internal rhyme and assonance, the stream of consciousness in which images collide. In MacNeice's earlier poetry the images often produce a kaleidoscopic whirl. At the same time, as he says of 'Snow', they are 'bang centre stage'. During the 1940s his approach to imagery, as to poetry in general, changed. 'After *The Earth Compels* I tired of tourism and after *Autumn Journal* I tired of journalism.' This involved 'a more structural use of imagery' which proved fundamental to the 'parable' poems of his last two collections. 'Charon' is a sustained example of 'the image that pinpoints in'. All the details of the journey converge on the image that incarnates its meaning:

> And there was the ferryman just as Virgil
> And Dante had seen him. He looked at us coldly
> And his eyes were dead and his hands on the oar
> Were black with obols and varicose veins
> Marbled his calves and he said to us coldly:
> If you want to die you will have to pay for it.

In a sense, the engagement of MacNeice's poetry with public crises was a long detour, the detour his generation had to make. The continuity between 'River in Spate' and 'Charon' excludes, as it were, the discursiveness of *Autumn Journal*. In each case MacNeice finds a strange rhythm to fit a strange symbolic situation. 'River in Spate' anticipates those later poems in which his preoccupation with time and motion either speeds up or slows down their rhythmic progress: for example, 'Variation on Heraclitus', 'Hold-up', 'Birthright'. In 'An Alphabet of Literary Prejudices' MacNeice writes:

> Verse is a precision instrument and owes its precision very largely to the many and subtle differences which an ordinary word can acquire from its place in a rhythmical scheme.

In MacNeice's later poetry the 'precision instrument' works with ever greater complexity. Here the full range of his classicist's rhetorical know-how, all his experiments with rhyme, refrain, assonance and stanzaic shape meet in a new synthesis. The lyric poem reaches a new frontier.

This selection favours the lyrical MacNeice. He was not to succeed in re-running the magnificent marathon of *Autumn Journal*. I have included little from *Ten Burnt Offerings* and *Autumn Sequel*. Like W. H. Auden, 'I do find them a bit dull.' If, as I have suggested, MacNeice's poetry began and continued as a reaction against darkness, then it might help to regard this dry period as an equinox when the tensions between light and darkness were too even. He was a poet of the solstice, of the uneven and unbalancing pull, at his best in his twenties and thirties and again after his fiftieth birthday. His penultimate collection, published in 1961, is entitled *Solstices*. It confirms creative recovery. The poems in *The Burning Perch* are poems of the winter solstice. The nightmares of childhood fuse with the real nightmare of growing older. But these poems are also powered by metaphysical urgency, and they incorporate a bleak view of the contemporary world. The early 1960s appear to MacNeice as 'evil' a time as the early 1930s: plastic, denatured, menaced by nuclear holocaust. In his commentary on *The Burning Perch* he observes:

> Fear and resentment seem here to be serving me in the same way as Yeats in his old age claimed to be served by 'lust and rage', and yet I had been equally fearful and resentful of the world we live in when I was writing *Solstices*.

MacNeice goes on to suggest that the 'sombreness' of *The Burning Perch* does not altogether negate his happier masks:

> I would venture the generalization that most of these poems are two-way affairs or at least spiral ones: even in the most evil picture the good things, like the sea in one of these poems, are still there round the corner.

There are many 'spirals' in his work. One way of tracing its genetic coding is to examine his love poetry. An image in 'Meeting Point' affirms love's victory over time:

> The bell was silent in the air
> Holding its inverted poise –
> Between the clang and clang a flower,
> A brazen calyx of no noise . . .

The life-denying bell is transformed into a symbol of life. This is an image that 'ripples out' – forward to 'The Introduction' where the lovers are 'introduced in a green grave'; backwards to MacNeice's first masterpiece 'Mayfly':

> But when this summer is over let us die together,
> I want always to be near your breasts.

These two beautiful lines disclose the nucleus of his imagination.

MacNeice's reputation was dulled by the dull stretches, then frozen by his premature death. And readers were slow to appreciate the astonishing breakthrough of his later poems. More broadly, to the Irish he has often seemed an exile, to the English a stranger. His Anglo-Irishness has not been properly understood on either side of the Irish Sea. In England critics still respond mainly to those bits of his work which superficially resemble Auden. As William T.

McKinnon puts it, he is assigned to 'a group of (political) poets, whose luminary was Somebody Else'. A new generation of poets from Northern Ireland has helped to change perspectives. They have picked up frequencies in his work which were inaudible in Dublin or London. Derek Mahon, who when still a schoolboy heard MacNeice as 'a familiar voice whispering in my ear', has learned particularly from the earlier work; Paul Muldoon from the techniques of the later. Muldoon's anthology *The Faber Book of Contemporary Irish Poetry* bears witness to MacNeice as a progenitor. He gives him more space than any other poet and in the epigraph-cum-prologue allows MacNeice's views on poetry to establish a perspective for the entire book. To speak for myself, rereading MacNeice for this selection I have again been overwhelmed and exhilarated. What other twentieth-century poet writing in English explores with such persistence and brilliance all that being alive can mean? Perhaps only Yeats. Certainly, when MacNeice honours Yeats's 'zest', he betrays a kinship. We can say of Louis MacNeice's poetry too: 'there is nearly always a leaping vitality – the vitality of Cleopatra waiting for the asp.'

Michael Longley
Belfast
March 1988

Trains in the Distance

Trains came threading quietly through my dozing childhood,
Gentle murmurs nosing through a summer quietude,
Drawing in and out, in and out, their smoky ribbons,
Parting now and then, and launching full-rigged galleons
And scrolls of smoke that hung in a shifting epitaph.
Then distantly the noise declined like a descending graph,
Sliding downhill gently to the bottom of the distance
(For now all things are there that all were here once);
And so we hardly noticed when that metal murmur came.
But it brought us assurance and comfort all the same,
And in the early night they soothed us to sleep,
And the chain of the rolling wheels bound us in deep
Till all was broken by that menace from the sea,
The steel-bosomed siren calling bitterly.

Poussin

In that Poussin the clouds are like golden tea,
And underneath the limbs flow rhythmically,
The cupids' blue feathers beat musically,
And we dally and dip our spoon in the golden tea.
The tea flows down the steps and up again,
An old-world fountain, pouring from sculptured lips,
And the chilly marble drop like sugar slips
And is lost in the dark gold depths, and the refrain
Of tea-leaves floats about and in and out,
And the motion is still as when one walks and the moon
Walks parallel but relations remain the same.
And thus we never reach the dregs of the cup,
Though we drink it up and drink it up and drink it up,
And thus we dally and dip our spoon.

River in Spate

The river falls and over the walls the coffins of cold funerals
Slide deep and sleep there in the close tomb of the pool,
And yellow waters lave the grave and pebbles pave its mortuary
And the river horses vault and plunge with their assault and battery,
And helter-skelter the coffins come and the drums beat and the
waters flow,
And the panther horses lift their hooves and paw and shift and draw
the bier,
The corpses blink in the rush of the river, and out of the water their
chins they tip
And quaff the gush and lip the draught and crook their heads and
crow,
Drowned and drunk with the cataract that carries them and buries
them
And silts them over and covers them and lilts and chuckles over their
bones;
The organ-tones that the winds raise will never pierce the water
ways,
So all they will hear is the fall of hooves and the distant shake of
harness,
And the beat of the bells on the horses' heads and the undertaker's
laughter,
And the murmur that will lose its strength and blur at length to
quietness,
And afterwards the minute heard descending, never ending heard,
And then the minute after and the minute after the minute after.

Mayfly

Barometer of my moods today, mayfly,
Up and down one among a million, one
The same at best as the rest of the jigging mayflies,
One only day of May alive beneath the sun.

The yokels tilt their pewters and the foam
Flowers in the sun beside the jewelled water.
Daughter of the South, call the sunbeams home
To nest between your breasts. The kingcups
Ephemeral are gay gulps of laughter.

Gulp of yellow merriment; cackle of ripples;
Lips of the river that pout and whisper round the reeds.
The mayfly flirting and posturing over the water
Goes up and down in the lift so many times for fun.

'When we are grown up we are sure to alter
Much for the better, to adopt solider creeds;
The kingcup will cease proffering his cup
And the foam will have blown from the beer and the heat no longer
                                                                        dance
And the lift lose fascination and the May
Change her tune to June – but the trouble with us mayflies
Is that we never have the chance to be grown up.'

They never have the chance, but what of time they have
They stretch out taut and thin and ringing clear;
So we, whose strand of life is not much more,
Let us too make our time elastic and
Inconsequently dance above the dazzling wave.

Nor put too much on the sympathy of things,
The dregs of drink, the dried cups of flowers,
The pathetic fallacy of the passing hours
When it is we who pass them – hours of stone,
Long rows of granite sphinxes looking on.

It is we who pass them, we the circus masters
Who make the mayflies dance, the lapwings lift their crests,
The show will soon shut down, its gay-rags gone,
But when this summer is over let us die together,
I want always to be near your breasts.

An Eclogue for Christmas

A. I meet you in an evil time.
B.   The evil bells
    Put out of our heads, I think, the thought of everything else.
A. The jaded calendar revolves,
    Its nuts need oil, carbon chokes the valves,
    The excess sugar of a diabetic culture
    Rotting the nerve of life and literature;
    Therefore when we bring out the old tinsel and frills
    To announce that Christ is born among the barbarous hills
    I turn to you whom a morose routine
    Saves from the mad vertigo of being what has been.
B. Analogue of me, you are wrong to turn to me,
    My country will not yield you any sanctuary,
    There is no pinpoint in any of the ordnance maps
    To save you when your towns and town-bred thoughts collapse,
    It is better to die *in situ* as I shall,
    One place is as bad as another. Go back where your instincts call
    And listen to the crying of the town-cats and the taxis again,
    Or wind your gramophone and eavesdrop on great men.
A. Jazz-weary of years of drums and Hawaiian guitar,
    Pivoting on the parquet I seem to have moved far
    From bombs and mud and gas, have stuttered on my feet
    Clinched to the streamlined and butter-smooth trulls of the elite,
    The lights irritating and gyrating and rotating in gauze –
    Pomade-dazzle, a slick beauty of gewgaws –
    I who was Harlequin in the childhood of the century,
    Posed by Picasso beside an endless opaque sea,
    Have seen myself sifted and splintered in broken facets,
    Tentative pencillings, endless liabilities, no assets,
    Abstractions scalpelled with a palette-knife
    Without reference to this particular life.
    And so it has gone on; I have not been allowed to be

Myself in flesh or face, but abstracting and dissecting me
They have made of me pure form, a symbol or a pastiche,
Stylized profile, anything but soul and flesh:
And that is why I turn this jaded music on
To forswear thought and become an automaton.

B. There are in the country also of whom I am afraid –
Men who put beer into a belly that is dead,
Women in the forties with terrier and setter who whistle and
swank
Over down and plough and Roman road and daisied bank,
Half-conscious that these barriers over which they stride
Are nothing to the barbed wire that has grown round their pride.

A. And two there are, as I drive in the city, who suddenly perturb –
The one sirening me to draw up by the kerb
The other, as I lean back, my right leg stretched creating speed,
Making me catch and stamp, the brakes shrieking, pull up dead:
She wears silk stockings taunting the winter wind,
He carries a white stick to mark that he is blind.

B. In the country they are still hunting, in the heavy shires
Greyness is on the fields and sunset like a line of pyres
Of barbarous heroes smoulders through the ancient air
Hazed with factory dust and, orange opposite, the moon's glare,
Goggling, yokel-stubborn through the iron trees,
Jeers at the end of us, our bland ancestral ease;
We shall go down like palaeolithic man
Before some new Ice Age or Genghiz Khan.

A. It is time for some new coinage, people have got so old,
Hacked and handled and shiny from pocketing they have made
bold
To think that each is himself through these accidents, being blind
To the fact that they are merely the counters of an unknown Mind.

B. A Mind that does not think, if such a thing can be,
Mechanical Reason, capricious Identity.
That I could be able to face this domination nor flinch –

A. The tin toys of the hawker move on the pavement inch by inch
Not knowing that they are wound up; it is better to be so
Than to be, like us, wound up and while running down to know –

B. But everywhere the pretence of individuality recurs –

A. Old faces frosted with powder and choked in furs.

B. The jutlipped farmer gazing over the humpbacked wall.

A. The commercial traveller joking in the urinal.

[5]

B. I think things draw to an end, the soil is stale.
A. And over-elaboration will nothing now avail,
   The street is up again, gas, electricity or drains,
   Ever-changing conveniences, nothing comfortable remains
   Un-improved, as flagging Rome improved villa and sewer
   (A sound-proof library and a stable temperature).
   Our street is up, red lights sullenly mark
   The long trench of pipes, iron guts in the dark,
   And not till the Goths again come swarming down the hill
   Will cease the clangour of the pneumatic drill.
   But yet there is beauty narcotic and deciduous
   In this vast organism grown out of us:
   On all the traffic-islands stand white globes like moons,
   The city's haze is clouded amber that purrs and croons,
   And tilting by the noble curve bus after tall bus comes
   With an osculation of yellow light, with a glory like chrysan-
                                                                themums.
B. The country gentry cannot change, they will die in their shoes
   From angry circumstance and moral self-abuse,
   Dying with a paltry fizzle they will prove their lives to be
   An ever-diluted drug, a spiritual tautology.
   They cannot live once their idols are turned out,
   None of them can endure, for how could they, possibly, without
   The flotsam of private property, pekinese and polyanthus,
   The good things which in the end turn to poison and pus,
   Without the bandy chairs and the sugar in the silver tongs
   And the inter-ripple and resonance of years of dinner-gongs?
   Or if they could find no more that cumulative proof
   In the rain dripping off the conservatory roof?
   What will happen when the only sanction the country-dweller
                                                                has –
A. What will happen to us, planked and panelled with jazz?
   Who go to the theatre where a black man dances like an eel,
   Where pink thighs flash like the spokes of a wheel, where we feel
   That we know in advance all the jogtrot and the cake-walk jokes,
   All the bumfun and the gags of the comedians in boaters and
                                                                toques,
   All the tricks of the virtuosos who invert the usual –
B. What will happen to us when the State takes down the manor
                                                                wall,
   When there is no more private shooting or fishing, when the trees
                                                                are all cut down,

When faces are all dials and cannot smile or frown –

A. What will happen when the sniggering machine-guns in the
                                    hands of the young men
   Are trained on every flat and club and beauty parlour and Father's
                                                    den?
   What will happen when our civilization like a long-pent balloon –

B. What will happen will happen; the whore and the buffoon
   Will come off best; no dreamers, they cannot lose their dream
   And are at least likely to be reinstated in the new regime.
   But one thing is not likely –

A.   Do not gloat over yourself,
   Do not be your own vulture; high on some mountain shelf
   Huddle the pitiless abstractions bald about the neck
   Who will descend when you crumple in the plains a wreck.
   Over the randy of the theatre and cinema I hear songs
   Unlike anything –

B.   The lady of the house poises the silver tongs
   And picks a lump of sugar, 'ne plus ultra' she says
   'I cannot do otherwise, even to prolong my days' –

A. I cannot do otherwise either, tonight I will book my seat –

B. I will walk about the farm-yard which is replete
   As with the smell of dung so with memories –

A. I will gorge myself to satiety with the oddities
   Of every artiste, official or amateur,
   Who has pleased me in my role of hero-worshipper
   Who has pleased me in my role of individual man –

B. Let us lie once more, say, 'What we think, we can'
   The old idealist lie –

A.   And for me before I die
   Let me go the round of the garish glare –

B.   And on the bare and high
   Places of England, the Wiltshire Downs and the Long Mynd
   Let the balls of my feet bounce on the turf, my face burn in the
                                                    wind
   My eyelashes stinging in the wind, and the sheep like grey stones
   Humble my human pretensions –

A.   Let the saxophones and the xylophones
   And the cult of every technical excellence, the miles of canvas in
                                              the galleries

And the canvas of the rich man's yacht snapping and tacking on
                                                        the seas
And the perfection of a grilled steak –
B.   Let all these so ephemeral things
Be somehow permanent like the swallow's tangent wings:
Goodbye to you, this day remember is Christmas, this morn
They say, interpret it your own way, Christ is born.

Eclogue by a Five-barred Gate

(Death and two Shepherds)

D. There is no way here, shepherds, read the wooden sign,
   Your road is a blind road, all this land is mine.
1. But your fields, mister, would do well for our sheep.
2. They could shelter from the sun where the low hills dip.
D. I have sheep of my own, see them over there.
1. There seems no nater in 'em, they look half dead.
2. They be no South Downs, they look so thin and bare.
D. More than half, shepherds, they are more than half dead.
   But where are your own flocks you have been so talking of?
1. Right here at our elbow –
2.   Or they *was* so just now.
D. That's right, shepherd, they was so just now.
   Your sheep are gone, they can't speak for you,
   I must have your credentials, sing me who you are.
1. I am a shepherd of the Theocritean breed,
   Been pasturing my songs, man and boy, this thirty year –
2. And for me too my pedigree acceptances
   Have multiplied beside the approved streams.
D. This won't do, shepherds, life is not like that,
   And when it comes to death I may say he is not like that.
   Have you never thought of Death?
1.   Only off and on,
   Thanatos in Greek, the accent proparoxytone –
2. That's not what he means, he means the thing behind the
                                                          word
   Same as took Alice White the time her had her third –
D. Cut out for once the dialect and the pedantry,
   I thought a shepherd was a poet –

[8]

1.   On his flute –
2.   On his oat –
D. I thought he was a poet and could quote the prices
   Of significant living and decent dying, could lay the rails level
                                         on the sleepers
   To carry the powerful train of abstruse thought –
1. What an idea!
2.   But certainly poets are sleepers,
   The sleeping beauty behind the many-coloured hedge –
D. All you do is burke the other and terrible beauty, all you do is
                                         hedge
   And shirk the inevitable issue, all you do
   Is shear your sheep to stop your ears.
   Poetry you think is only the surface vanity,
   The painted nails, the hips narrowed by fashion,
   The hooks and eyes of words; but it is not that only,
   And it is not only the curer sitting by the wayside,
   Phials on his trestle, his palms grown thin as wafers
   With blessing the anonymous heads;
   And poetry is not only the bridging of two-banked rivers.
2. Who ever heard of a river without a further bank?
D. You two never heard of it.
   Tell me now, I have heard the cuckoo, there is tar on your
                                         shoes,
   I surmise that spring is here –
2.   Spring be here truly,
   On Bank Holiday I wore canvas shoes,
   Could feel the earth –
D.   And that being so, tell me
   Don't you ever feel old?
2.   There's a question now.
1. It is a question we all have to answer,
   And I may say that when I smell the beans or hear the thrush
   I feel a wave intensely bitter-sweet and topped with silver –
D. There you go again, your self-congratulation
   Blunts all edges, insulates with wool,
   No spark of reality possible.
   Can't you peel off for even a moment that conscious face?
   All time is not your tear-off jotter, you cannot afford to scribble
   So many so false answers.
   This escapism of yours is blasphemy,

                          [9]

An immortal cannot blaspheme for one way or another
His trivialities will pattern in the end;
But for you your privilege and panic is to be mortal
And with Here and Now for your anvil
You must strike while the iron is hot –

2.   He is an old man,
That is why he talks so.
D.   Can't you understand me?
Look, I will set you a prize like any of your favourites,
Like any Tityrus or tired Damon;
Sing me, each in turn, what dream you had last night
And if either's dream rings true, to him I will open my gate.
2. Ho, here's talking.
1.   Let me collect myself.
D. Collect yourself in time for if you win my prize –
2. I'm going to sing first, I had a rare dream.
1. Your dream is nothing –
D.   The more nothing the better.
1. My dream will word well –
2.   But not wear well –
D. No dreams wear at all as dreams.
Water appears tower only while in well –
All from the same comes, the same drums sound
In the pulsation of all the bulging suns,
And no clock whatever, while winding or running down,
Makes any difference to time however the long-legged
                                       weights
Straggle down the cottage wall or the child grows leggy too –
1. I do not like your talking.
2.   It give giddiness
Like the thrumming of the telephone wires in an east wind
With the bellyache and headache and nausea.
D. It is not my nature to talk, so sing your pieces
And I will try, what is repugnant too, to listen.
1. Last night as the bearded lips of sleep
Closed with the slightest sigh on me and I sank through the
                                 blue soft caves
Picked with light delicate as the chink of coins
Or stream on the pebbles I was caught by hands
And a face was swung in my eyes like a lantern
Swinging on the neck of a snake.

And that face I knew to be God and I woke,
And now I come to look at yours, stranger,
There is something in the lines of it –
D.   Your dream, shepherd,
Is good enough of its kind. Now let us hear yours.
2. Well, I dreamt it was a hot day, the territorials
Were out on melting asphalt under the howitzers,
The brass music bounced on the houses. Come
I heard cry as it were a water-nymph, come and fulfil me
And I sped floating, my feet plashing in the tops of the wheat
But my eyes were blind,
I found her with my hands lying on the drying hay,
Wet heat in the deeps of the hay as my hand delved,
And I possessed her, gross and good like the hay,
And she went and my eyes regained sight and the sky was full
                                                of ladders
Angels ascending and descending with a shine like mackerel –
Now I come to tell it it sounds nonsense.
D. Thank you, gentlemen, these two dreams are good,
Better than your daytime madrigals.
If you really wish I will give you both the prize,
But take another look at my land before you choose it.
1. It looks colder now.
2.   The sheep have not moved.
1. I have a fancy there is no loving there
Even among sheep.
D.   They do not breed or couple.
1 & 2. And what about us, shall we enjoy it there?
D. *Enjoy what where?*
2.   Why, life in your land.
D. I will open this gate that you may see for yourselves.
1. You go first.
2.   Well, you come too.
1 & 2. We will go together to these pastures new . . .
D. So; they are gone; life in my land . . .
There is no life as there is no land.
They are gone and I am alone
With a gate the façade of a mirage.

[11]

Valediction

Their verdure dare not show . . . their verdure dare not show . . .
Cant and randy – the seals' heads bobbing in the tide-flow
Between the islands, sleek and black and irrelevant
They cannot depose logically what they want:
Died by gunshot under borrowed pennons,
Sniped from the wet gorse and taken by the limp fins
And slung like a dead seal in a boghole, beaten up
By peasants with long lips and the whisky-drinker's cough.
Park your car in the city of Dublin, see Sackville Street
Without the sandbags in the old photos, meet
The statues of the patriots, history never dies,
At any rate in Ireland, arson and murder are legacies
Like old rings hollow-eyed without their stones
Dumb talismans.
See Belfast, devout and profane and hard,
Built on reclaimed mud, hammers playing in the shipyard,
Time punched with holes like a steel sheet, time
Hardening the faces, veneering with a grey and speckled rime
The faces under the shawls and caps:
This was my mother-city, these my paps.
Country of callous lava cooled to stone,
Of minute sodden haycocks, of ship-sirens' moan,
Of falling intonations – I would call you to book
I would say to you, Look;
I would say, This is what you have given me
Indifference and sentimentality
A metallic giggle, a fumbling hand,
A heart that leaps to a fife band:
Set these against your water-shafted air
Of amethyst and moonstone, the horses' feet like bells of hair
Shambling beneath the orange cart, the beer-brown spring
Guzzling between the heather, the green gush of Irish spring.
Cursèd be he that curses his mother. I cannot be
Anyone else than what this land engendered me:
In the back of my mind are snips of white, the sails
Of the Lough's fishing-boats, the bellropes lash their tails
When I would peal my thoughts, the bells pull free –
Memory in apostasy.
I would tot up my factors

But who can stand in the way of his soul's steam-tractors?
I can say Ireland is hooey, Ireland is
A gallery of fake tapestries,
But I cannot deny my past to which my self is wed,
The woven figure cannot undo its thread.
On a cardboard lid I saw when I was four
Was the trade-mark of a hound and a round tower,
And that was Irish glamour, and in the cemetery
Sham Celtic crosses claimed our individuality,
And my father talked about the West where years back
He played hurley on the sands with a stick of wrack.
Park your car in Killarney, buy a souvenir
Of green marble or black bog-oak, run up to Clare,
Climb the cliff in the postcard, visit Galway city,
Romanticize on our Spanish blood, leave ten per cent of pity
Under your plate for the emigrant,
Take credit for our sanctity, our heroism and our sterile want
Columba Kevin and briny Brandan the accepted names,
Wolfe Tone and Grattan and Michael Collins the accepted names,
Admire the suavity with which the architect
Is rebuilding the burnt mansion, recollect
The palmy days of the Horse Show, swank your fill,
But take the Holyhead boat before you pay the bill;
Before you face the consequence
Of inbred soul and climatic maleficence
And pay for the trick beauty of a prism
In drug-dull fatalism.
I will exorcize my blood
And not to have my baby-clothes my shroud
I will acquire an attitude not yours
And become as one of your holiday visitors,
And however often I may come
Farewell, my country, and in perpetuum;
Whatever desire I catch when your wind scours my face
I will take home and put in a glass case
And merely look on
At each new fantasy of badge and gun.
Frost will not touch the hedge of fuchsias,
The land will remain as it was,
But no abiding content can grow out of these minds
Fuddled with blood, always caught by blinds;

[13]

The eels go up the Shannon over the great dam;
You cannot change a response by giving it a new name.
Fountain of green and blue curling in the wind
I must go east and stay, not looking behind,
Not knowing on which day the mist is blanket-thick
Nor when sun quilts the valley and quick
Winging shadows of white clouds pass
Over the long hills like a fiddle's phrase.
If I were a dog of sunlight I would bound
From Phoenix Park to Achill Sound,
Picking up the scent of a hundred fugitives
That have broken the mesh of ordinary lives,
But being ordinary too I must in course discuss
What we mean to Ireland or Ireland to us;
I have to observe milestone and curio
The beaten buried gold of an old king's bravado,
Falsetto antiquities, I have to gesture,
Take part in, or renounce, each imposture;
Therefore I resign, goodbye the chequered and the quiet hills
The gaudily-striped Atlantic, the linen-mills
That swallow the shawled file, the black moor where half
A turf-stack stands like a ruined cenotaph;
Goodbye your hens running in and out of the white house
Your absent-minded goats along the road, your black cows
Your greyhounds and your hunters beautifully bred
Your drums and your dolled-up Virgins and your ignorant dead.

Belfast

The hard cold fire of the northerner
Frozen into his blood from the fire in his basalt
Glares from behind the mica of his eyes
And the salt carrion water brings him wealth.

Down there at the end of the melancholy lough
Against the lurid sky over the stained water
Where hammers clang murderously on the girders
Like crucifixes the gantries stand.

And in the marble stores rubber gloves like polyps
Cluster; celluloid, painted ware, glaring
Metal patents, parchment lampshades, harsh
Attempts at buyable beauty.

In the porch of the chapel before the garish Virgin
A shawled factory-woman as if shipwrecked there
Lies a bunch of limbs glimpsed in the cave of gloom
By us who walk in the street so buoyantly and glib.

Over which country of cowled and haunted faces
The sun goes down with a banging of Orange drums
While the male kind murders each its woman
To whose prayer for oblivion answers no Madonna.

Birmingham

Smoke from the train-gulf hid by hoardings blunders upward, the
                                                    brakes of cars
Pipe as the policeman pivoting round raises his flat hand, bars
With his figure of a monolith Pharaoh the queue of fidgety machines
(Chromium dogs on the bonnet, faces behind the triplex screens).
Behind him the streets run away between the proud glass of shops,
Cubical scent-bottles artificial legs arctic foxes and electric mops,
But beyond this centre the slumward vista thins like a diagram:
There, unvisited, are Vulcan's forges who doesn't care a tinker's
                                                    damn.

Splayed outwards through the suburbs houses, houses for rest
Seducingly rigged by the builder, half-timbered houses with lips
                                                    pressed
So tightly and eyes staring at the traffic through bleary haws
And only a six-inch grip of the racing earth in their concrete claws;
In these houses men as in a dream pursue the Platonic Forms
With wireless and cairn terriers and gadgets approximating to the
                                                    fickle norms
And endeavour to find God and score one over the neighbour
By climbing tentatively upward on jerry-built beauty and sweated
                                                    labour.

The lunch hour: the shops empty, shopgirls' faces relax
Diaphanous as green glass, empty as old almanacs
As incoherent with ticketed gewgaws tiered behind their heads
As the Burne-Jones windows in St Philip's broken by crawling leads;
Insipid colour, patches of emotion, Saturday thrills
(This theatre is sprayed with 'June') – the gutter take our old
                                                    playbills,
Next week-end it is likely in the heart's funfair we shall pull
Strong enough on the handle to get back our money; or at any rate it
                                                    is possible.

On shining lines the trams like vast sarcophagi move
Into the sky, plum after sunset, merging to duck's egg, barred with
                                                    mauve
Zeppelin clouds, and Pentecost-like the cars' headlights bud
Out from sideroads and the traffic signals, crème-de-menthe or bull's
                                                    blood,

[16]

Tell one to stop, the engine gently breathing, or to go on
To where like black pipes of organs in the frayed and fading zone
Of the West the factory chimneys on sullen sentry will all night wait
To call, in the harsh morning, sleep-stupid faces through the daily
                                                                gate.

Turf-stacks

Among these turf-stacks graze no iron horses
Such as stalk, such as champ in towns and the soul of crowds,
Here is no mass-production of neat thoughts
No canvas shrouds for the mind nor any black hearses:
The peasant shambles on his boots like hooves
Without thinking at all or wanting to run in grooves.

But those who lack the peasant's conspirators,
The tawny mountain, the unregarded buttress,
Will feel the need of a fortress against ideas and against the
Shuddering insidious shock of the theory-vendors,
The little sardine men crammed in a monster toy
Who tilt their aggregate beast against our crumbling Troy.

For we are obsolete who like the lesser things
Who play in corners with looking-glasses and beads;
It is better we should go quickly, go into Asia
Or any other tunnel where the world recedes,
Or turn blind wantons like the gulls who scream
And rip the edge off any ideal or dream.

Spring Voices

The small householder now comes out warily
Afraid of the barrage of sun that shouts cheerily,
Spring is massing forces, birds wink in air,
The battlemented chestnuts volley green fire,
The pigeons banking on the wind, the hoots of cars,
Stir him to run wild, gamble on horses, buy cigars;
Joy lies before him to be ladled and lapped from his hand –
Only that behind him, in the shade of his villa, memories stand
Breathing on his neck and muttering that all this has happened
                                                            before,
Keep the wind out, cast no clout, try no unwarranted jaunts untried
                                                            before,
But let the spring slide by nor think to board its car
For it rides West to where the tangles of scrap-iron are;
Do not walk, these voices say, between the bucking clouds alone
Or you may loiter into a suddenly howling crater, or fall, jerked back,
                                         garrotted by the sun.

Nature Morte

(Even so it is not so easy to be dead)

As those who are not athletic at breakfast day by day
Employ and enjoy the sinews of others vicariously,
Shielded by the upheld journal from their dream-puncturing wives
And finding in the printed word a multiplication of their lives,
So we whose senses give us things misfelt and misheard
Turn also, for our adjustment, to the pretentious word
Which stabilizes the light on the sun-fondled trees
And, by photographing our ghosts, claims to put us at our ease;
Yet even so, no matter how solid and staid we contrive
Our reconstructions, even a still life is alive
And in your Chardin the appalling unrest of the soul
Exudes from the dried fish and the brown jug and the bowl.

Sunday Morning

Down the road someone is practising scales,
The notes like little fishes vanish with a wink of tails,
Man's heart expands to tinker with his car
For this is Sunday morning, Fate's great bazaar;
Regard these means as ends, concentrate on this Now,
And you may grow to music or drive beyond Hindhead anyhow,
Take corners on two wheels until you go so fast
That you can clutch a fringe or two of the windy past,
That you can abstract this day and make it to the week of time
A small eternity, a sonnet self-contained in rhyme.

But listen, up the road, something gulps, the church spire
Opens its eight bells out, skulls' mouths which will not tire
To tell how there is no music or movement which secures
Escape from the weekday time. Which deadens and endures.

August

The shutter of time darkening ceaselessly
Has whisked away the foam of may and elder
And I realize how now, as every year before,
Once again the gay months have eluded me.

For the mind, by nature stagey, welds its frame
Tomb-like around each little world of a day;
We jump from picture to picture and cannot follow
The living curve that is breathlessly the same.

While the lawn-mower sings moving up and down
Spirting its little fountain of vivid green,
I, like Poussin, make a still-bound fête of us
Suspending every noise, of insect or machine.

Garlands at a set angle that do not slip,
Theatrically (and as if for ever) grace
You and me and the stone god in the garden
And Time who also is shown with a stone face.

But all this is a dilettante's lie,
Time's face is not stone nor still his wings;
Our mind, being dead, wishes to have time die
For we, being ghosts, cannot catch hold of things.

Morning Sun

Shuttles of trains going north, going south, drawing threads of blue,
The shining of the lines of trams like swords,
Thousands of posters asserting a monopoly of the good, the
                                        beautiful, the true,
Crowds of people all in the vocative, you and you,
The haze of the morning shot with words.

Yellow sun comes white off the wet streets but bright
Chromium yellows in the gay sun's light,
Filleted sun streaks the purple mist,
Everything is kissed and reticulated with sun
Scooped-up and cupped in the open fronts of shops
And bouncing on the traffic which never stops.

And the street fountain blown across the square
Rainbow-trellises the air and sunlight blazons
The red butcher's and scrolls of fish on marble slabs,
Whistled bars of music crossing silver sprays
And horns of cars, touché, touché, rapiers' retort, a moving cage,
A turning page of shine and sound, the day's maze.

But when the sun goes out, the streets go cold, the hanging meat
And tiers of fish are colourless and merely dead,
And the hoots of cars neurotically repeat and the tiptoed feet
Of women hurry and falter whose faces are dead;
And I see in the air but not belonging there
The blown grey powder of the fountain grey as the ash
That forming on a cigarette covers the red.

Train to Dublin

Our half-thought thoughts divide in sifted wisps
Against the basic facts repatterned without pause,
I can no more gather my mind up in my fist
Than the shadow of the smoke of this train upon the grass —
This is the way that animals' lives pass.

The train's rhythm never relents, the telephone posts
Go striding backwards like the legs of time to where
In a Georgian house you turn at the carpet's edge
Turning a sentence while, outside my window here,
The smoke makes broken queries in the air.

The train keeps moving and the rain holds off,
I count the buttons on the seat, I hear a shell
Held hollow to the ear, the mere
Reiteration of integers, the bell
That tolls and tolls, the monotony of fear.

At times we are doctrinaire, at times we are frivolous,
Plastering over the cracks, a gesture making good,
But the strength of us does not come out of us.
It is we, I think, are the idols and it is God
Has set us up as men who are painted wood,

And the trains carry us about. But not consistently so,
For during a tiny portion of our lives we are not in trains,
The idol living for a moment, not muscle-bound
But walking freely through the slanting rain,
Its ankles wet, its grimace relaxed again.

All over the world people are toasting the King,
Red lozenges of light as each one lifts his glass,
But I will not give you any idol or idea, creed or king,
I give you the incidental things which pass
Outward through space exactly as each was.

I give you the disproportion between labour spent
And joy at random; the laughter of the Galway sea
Juggling with spars and bones irresponsibly,
I give you the toy Liffey and the vast gulls,
I give you fuchsia hedges and whitewashed walls.

I give you the smell of Norman stone, the squelch
Of bog beneath your boots, the red bog-grass,
The vivid chequer of the Antrim hills, the trough of dark
Golden water for the cart-horses, the brass
Belt of serene sun upon the lough.

And I give you the faces, not the permanent masks,
But the faces balanced in the toppling wave –
His glint of joy in cunning as the farmer asks
Twenty per cent too much, or a girl's, forgetting to be suave,
A tiro choosing stuffs, preferring mauve.

And I give you the sea and yet again the sea's
Tumultuous marble,
With Thor's thunder or taking his ease akimbo,
Lumbering torso, but finger-tips a marvel
Of surgeon's accuracy.

I would like to give you more but I cannot hold
This stuff within my hands and the train goes on;
I know that there are further syntheses to which,
As you have perhaps, people at last attain
And find that they are rich and breathing gold.

Wolves

I do not want to be reflective any more
Envying and despising unreflective things
Finding pathos in dogs and undeveloped handwriting
And young girls doing their hair and all the castles of sand
Flushed by the children's bedtime, level with the shore.

The tide comes in and goes out again, I do not want
To be always stressing either its flux or its permanence,
I do not want to be a tragic or philosophic chorus
But to keep my eye only on the nearer future
And after that let the sea flow over us.

Come then all of you, come closer, form a circle,
Join hands and make believe that joined
Hands will keep away the wolves of water
Who howl along our coast. And be it assumed
That no one hears them among the talk and laughter.

Snow

The room was suddenly rich and the great bay-window was
Spawning snow and pink roses against it
Soundlessly collateral and incompatible:
World is suddener than we fancy it.

World is crazier and more of it than we think,
Incorrigibly plural. I peel and portion
A tangerine and spit the pips and feel
The drunkenness of things being various.

And the fire flames with a bubbling sound for world
Is more spiteful and gay than one supposes –
On the tongue on the eyes on the ears in the palms of one's hands –
There is more than glass between the snow and the huge roses.

Carrickfergus

I was born in Belfast between the mountain and the gantries
    To the hooting of lost sirens and the clang of trams:
Thence to Smoky Carrick in County Antrim
    Where the bottle-neck harbour collects the mud which jams

The little boats beneath the Norman castle,
    The pier shining with lumps of crystal salt;
The Scotch Quarter was a line of residential houses
    But the Irish Quarter was a slum for the blind and halt.

The brook ran yellow from the factory stinking of chlorine,
    The yarn-mill called its funeral cry at noon;
Our lights looked over the lough to the lights of Bangor
    Under the peacock aura of a drowning moon.

The Norman walled this town against the country
    To stop his ears to the yelping of his slave
And built a church in the form of a cross but denoting
    The list of Christ on the cross in the angle of the nave.

I was the rector's son, born to the anglican order,
    Banned for ever from the candles of the Irish poor;
The Chichesters knelt in marble at the end of a transept
    With ruffs about their necks, their portion sure.

The war came and a huge camp of soldiers
    Grew from the ground in sight of our house with long
Dummies hanging from gibbets for bayonet practice
    And the sentry's challenge echoing all day long;

A Yorkshire terrier ran in and out by the gate-lodge
    Barred to civilians, yapping as if taking affront:
Marching at ease and singing 'Who Killed Cock Robin?'
    The troops went out by the lodge and off to the Front.

The steamer was camouflaged that took me to England –
    Sweat and khaki in the Carlisle train;
I thought that the war would last for ever and sugar
    Be always rationed and that never again

Would the weekly papers not have photos of sandbags
  And my governess not make bandages from moss
And people not have maps above the fireplace
  With flags on pins moving across and across –

Across the hawthorn hedge the noise of bugles,
  Flares across the night,
Somewhere on the lough was a prison ship for Germans,
  A cage across their sight.

I went to school in Dorset, the world of parents
  Contracted into a puppet world of sons
Far from the mill girls, the smell of porter, the salt-mines
  And the soldiers with their guns.

Eclogue from Iceland

Scene: The Arnarvatn Heath. Craven, Ryan and the ghost of Grettir. Voice from Europe.

R. This is the place, Craven, the end of our way;
Hobble the horses, we have had a long day.

C. The night is closing like a fist
And the long glacier lost in mist.

R. Few folk come this time of year.
What are those limping steps I hear?

C. Look, there he is coming now.
We shall have some company anyhow.

R. It must be the mist – he looks so big;
He is walking lame in the left leg.

G. Good evening, strangers. So you too
Are on the run? I welcome you.
I am Grettir Asmundson,
Dead many years. My day is done.
But you whose day is sputtering yet –
I forget . . . What did I say?
We forget when we are dead
The blue and red, the grey and gay.
Your day spits with a damp wick,
Will fizzle out if you're not quick.
Men have been chilled to death who kissed
Wives of mist, forgetting their own
Kind who live out of the wind.
My memory goes, goes – Tell me
Are there men now whose compass leads
Them always down forbidden roads?
Greedy young men who take their pick
Of what they want but have no luck;
Who leap the toothed and dour crevasse
Of death on a sardonic phrase?
You with crowsfeet round your eyes
How are things where you come from?

C. Things are bad. There is no room
To move at ease, to stretch or breed –

G. And you with the burglar's underlip
In your land do things stand well?

[26]

R. In my land nothing stands at all
   But some fly high and some lie low.
G. Too many people. My memory will go,
   Lose itself in the hordes of modern people.
   Memory is words; we remember what others
   Say and record of ourselves – stones with the runes.
   Too many people – sandstorm over the words.
   Is your land also an island?
   There is only hope for people who live upon islands
   Where the Lowest Common labels will not stick
   And the unpolluted hills will hold your echo.
R. I come from an island, Ireland, a nation
   Built upon violence and morose vendettas.
   My diehard countrymen like drayhorses
   Drag their ruin behind them.
   Shooting straight in the cause of crooked thinking
   Their greed is sugared with pretence of public spirit.
   From all which I am an exile.
C. Yes, we are exiles,
   Gad the world for comfort.
   This Easter I was in Spain before the Civil War
   Gobbling the tripper's treats, the local colour,
   Storks over Avila, the coffee-coloured waters of Ronda,
   The comedy of the bootblacks in the cafés,
   The legless beggars in the corridors of the trains,
   Dominoes on marble tables, the architecture
   Moorish mudejar Churrigueresque,
   The bullfight – the banderillas like Christmas candles,
   And the scrawled hammer and sickle:
   It was all copy – impenetrable surface.
   I did not look for the sneer beneath the surface
   Why should I trouble, an addict to oblivion
   Running away from the gods of my own hearth
   With no intention of finding gods elsewhere?
R. And so we came to Iceland –
C. Our latest joyride.
G. And what have you found in Iceland?
C. What have we found? More copy, more surface,
   Vignettes as they call them, dead flowers in an album –
   The harmoniums in the farms, the fine-bread and pancakes,
   The pot of ivy trained across the window,

[27]

Children in gumboots, girls in black berets.

R. And dead craters and angled crags.

G. The crags which saw me jockey doom for twenty
Years from one cold hide-out to another;
The last of the saga heroes
Who had not the wisdom of Njal or the beauty of Gunnar
I was the doomed tough, disaster kept me witty;
Being born the surly jack, the ne'er-do-well, the loiterer
Hard blows exalted me.
When the man of will and muscle achieves the curule chair
He turns to a bully; better is his lot as outlaw
A wad of dried fish in his belt, a snatch of bilberries
And riding the sullen landscape far from friends
Through the jungle of lava, dales of frozen fancy
Fording the gletcher, ducking the hard hail,
And across the easy pastures, never stopping
To rest among the celandines and bogcotton.
Under a curse I would see eyes in the night,
Always had to move on; craving company
In the end I lived on an island with two others.
To fetch fire I swam the crinkled fjord,
The crags were alive with ravens whose low croak
Told my ears what filtered in my veins –
The sense of doom. I wore it gracefully,
The fatal clarity that would not budge
But without false pride in martyrdom. For I,
Joker and dressy, held no mystic's pose,
Not wishing to die preferred the daily goods
The horse-fight, women's thighs, a joint of meat.

C. But this dyspeptic age of ingrown cynics
Wakes in the morning with a coated tongue
And whets itself laboriously to labour
And wears a blasé face in the face of death.
Who risk their lives neither to fill their bellies
Nor to avenge an affront nor grab a prize
But out of bravado or to divert ennui
Driving fast cars and climbing foreign mountains.
Outside the delicatessen shop the hero
With his ribbons and his empty pinned-up sleeve
Cadges for money while with turned-up collars
His comrades blow through brass the Londonderry Air

And silken legs and swinging buttocks advertise
The sale of little cardboard flags on pins.

G. Us too they sold
The women and the men with many sheep.
Graft and aggression, legal prevarication
Drove out the best of us,
Secured long life to only the sly and the dumb
To those who would not say what they really thought
But got their ends through pretended indifference
And through the sweat and blood of thralls and hacks
Cheating the poor men of their share of drift
The whale on Kaldbak in the starving winter.

R. And so today at Grimsby men whose lives
Are warped in Arctic trawlers load and unload
The shining tons of fish to keep the lords
Of the market happy with cigars and cars.

C. What is that music in the air –
Organ-music coming from far?

R. Honeyed music – it sounds to me
Like the Wurlitzer in the Gaiety.

G. I do not hear anything at all.

C. Imagine the purple light on the stage.

R. The melting moment of a stinted age

C. The pause before the film again
Bursts in a shower of golden rain.

G. I do not hear anything at all.

C. We shall be back there soon, to stand in queues
For entertainment and to work at desks,
To browse round counters of dead books, to pore
On picture catalogues and Soho menus,
To preen ourselves on the reinterpretation
Of the words of obsolete interpreters,
Collate delete their faded lives like texts,
Admire Flaubert, Cézanne – the tortured artists –
And leaning forward to knock out our pipes
Into the fire protest that art is good
And gives a meaning and a slant to life.

G. The dark is falling. Soon the air
Will stare with eyes, the stubborn ghost
Who cursed me when I threw him. Must
The ban go on for ever? I,

A ghost myself, have no claim now to die.
R. Now I hear the music again –
Strauss and roses – hear it plain.
The sweet confetti of music falls
From the high Corinthian capitals.
C. Her head upon his shoulder lies. . . .
Blend to the marrow as the music dies.
G. Brought up to the rough-house we took offence quickly
Were sticklers for pride, paid for it as outlaws –
C. Like Cavalcanti whose hot blood lost him Florence
R. Or the Wild Geese of Ireland in Mid-Europe.
Let us thank God for valour in abstraction
For those who go their own way, will not kiss
The arse of law and order nor compound
For physical comfort at the price of pride:
Soldiers of fortune, renegade artists, rebels and sharpers
Whose speech not cramped to Yea and Nay explodes
In crimson oaths like peonies, who brag
Because they prefer to taunt the mask of God,
Bid him unmask and die in the living lightning.
What is that voice maundering, meandering?
VOICE. Blues . . . blues . . . high heels and manicured hands
Always self-conscious of the vanity bag
And puritan painted lips that abnegate desire
And say 'we do not care' . . . 'we do not care' –
I don't care always in the air
Give my hips a shake always on the make
Always on the mend coming around the bend
Always on the dance with an eye to the main
Chance, always taking the floor again –
C. There was Tchekov,
His haemorrhages drove him out of Moscow
The life he loved, not born to it, who thought
That when the windows blurred with smoke and talk
So that no one could see out, then conversely
The giants of frost and satans of the peasant
Could not look in, impose the evil eye.
R. There was MacKenna
Spent twenty years translating Greek philosophy
Ill and tormented, unwilling to break contract,
A brilliant talker who left

The salon for the solo flight of Mind.
G. There was Onund Treefoot
Came late and lame to Iceland, made his way
Even though the land was bad and the neighbours jealous.
C. There was that dancer
Who danced the War, then falling into coma
Went with hunched shoulders through the ivory gate.
R. There was Connolly
Vilified now by the gangs of Catholic Action.
G. There was Egil
Hero and miser who when dying blind
Would have thrown his money among the crowd to hear
The whole world scuffle for his hoarded gold.
C. And there were many
Whose commonsense or sense of humour or mere
Desire for self-assertion won them through
R. But not to happiness. Though at intervals
They paused in sunlight for a moment's fusion
With friends or nature till the cynical wind
Blew the trees pale –
VOICE.   Blues, blues, sit back, relax
Let your self-pity swell with the music and clutch
Your tiny lavendered fetishes. Who cares
If floods depopulate China? I don't care
Always in the air sitting among the stars
Among the electric signs among the imported wines
Always on the spree climbing the forbidden tree
Tossing the peel of the apple over my shoulder
To see it form the initials of a new intrigue
G. Runes and runes which no one could decode
R. Wrong numbers on the phone – she never answered.
C. And from the romantic grille (Spanish baroque)
Only the eyes looked out which I see now.
G. You see them now?
C.   But seen before as well.
G. And many times to come, be sure of that.
R. I know them too
These eyes which hang in the northern mist, the brute
Stare of stupidity and hate, the most
Primitive and false of oracles.

c.   The eyes
       That glide like snakes behind a thousand masks –
       All human faces fit them, here or here:
       Dictator, bullying schoolboy or common lout,
       Acquisitive women, financiers, invalids,
       Are capable all of that compelling stare
       Stare which betrays the cosmic purposelessness
       The nightmare noise of the scythe upon the hone,
       Time sharpening his blade among high rocks alone.
r.   The face that fate hangs as a figurehead
       Above the truncheon or the nickelled death.
g.   I won the fall. Though cursed for it, I won.
c.   Which is why we honour you who working from
       The common premises did not end with many
       In the blind alley where the trek began.
g.   Though the open road is hard with frost and dark.
voice. Hot towels for the men, mud packs for the women
       Will smooth the puckered minutes of your lives.
       I offer you each a private window, a view
       (The leper window reveals a church of lepers).
r.   Do you believe him?
c.   I don't know.
       Do you believe him?
g.   No.
       You cannot argue with the eyes or voice;
       Argument will frustrate you till you die
       But go your own way, give the voice the lie,
       Outstare the inhuman eyes. That is the way.
       Go back to where you came from and do not keep
       Crossing the road to escape them, do not avoid the ambush,
       Take sly detours, but ride the pass direct.
c.   But the points of axes shine from the scrub, the odds
       Are dead against us. There are the lures of women
       Who, half alive, invite to a fuller life
       And never loving would be loved by others.
r.   Who fortify themselves in pasteboard castles
       And plant their beds with the cast-out toys of children,
       Dead pines with tinsel fruits, nursery beliefs
       And South Sea Island trinkets. Watch their years
       The permutations of lapels and gussets,
       Of stuffs – georgette or velvet or corduroy –

Of hats and eye-veils, of shoes, lizard or suede,
Of bracelets, milk or coral, of zip bags
Of compacts, lipstick, eyeshade and coiffures
All tributary to the wished ensemble,
The carriage of body that belies the soul.

c. And there are the men who appear to be men of sense,
Good company and dependable in a crisis,
Who yet are ready to plug you as you drink
Like dogs who bite from fear; for fear of germs
Putting on stamps by licking the second finger,
For fear of opinion overtipping in bars,
For fear of thought studying stupefaction.
It is the world which these have made where dead
Greek words sprout out in tin on sallow walls –
Clinic or polytechnic – a world of slums
Where any day now may see the Gadarene swine
Rush down the gullets of the London tubes
When the enemy, x or y, let loose their gas.

g. My friends, hounded like me, I tell you still
Go back to where you belong. I could have fled
To the Hebrides or Orkney, been rich and famous,
Preferred to assert my rights in my own country,
Mine which were hers for every country stands
By the sanctity of the individual will.

r. Yes, he is right.

c.   But we have not his strength

r. Could only abase ourselves before the wall
Of shouting flesh

c.   Could only offer our humble
Deaths to the unknown god, unknown but worshipped,
Whose voice calls in the sirens of destroyers.

g. Minute your gesture but it must be made –
Your hazard, your act of defiance and hymn of hate,
Hatred of hatred, assertion of human values,
Which is now your only duty.

c. Is it our only duty?

g.   Yes, my friends.
What did you say? The night falls now and I
Must beat the dales to chase my remembered acts.
Yes, my friends, it is your only duty.
And, it may be added, it is your only chance.

[33]

Postscript to Iceland

for W. H. Auden

Now the winter nights begin
Lonely comfort walls me in;
So before the memory slip
I review our Iceland trip –

Not for me romantic nor
Idyll on a mythic shore
But a fancy turn, you know,
Sandwiched in a graver show.

Down in Europe Seville fell,
Nations germinating hell,
The Olympic games were run –
Spots upon the Aryan sun.

And the don in me set forth
How the landscape of the north
Had educed the saga style
Plodding forward mile by mile.

And the don in you replied
That the North begins inside,
Our ascetic guts require
Breathers from the Latin fire.

So although no ghost was scotched
We were happy while we watched
Ravens from their walls of shale
Cruise around the rotting whale,

Watched the sulphur basins boil,
Loops of steam uncoil and coil,
While the valley fades away
To a sketch of Judgment Day.

So we rode and joked and smoked
With no miracles evoked,
With no levitations won
In the thin unreal sun;

In that island never found
Visions blossom from the ground,
No conversions like St Paul,
No great happenings at all.

Holidays should be like this,
Free from over-emphasis,
Time for soul to stretch and spit
Before the world comes back on it,

Before the chimneys row on row
Sneer in smoke, 'We told you so'
And the fog-bound sirens call
Ruin to the long sea-wall.

Rows of books around me stand,
Fence me round on either hand;
Through that forest of dead words
I would hunt the living birds –

Great black birds that fly alone
Slowly through a land of stone,
And the gulls who weave a free
Quilt of rhythm on the sea.

Here in Hampstead I sit late
Nights which no one shares and wait
For the phone to ring or for
Unknown angels at the door;

Better were the northern skies
Than this desert in disguise –
Rugs and cushions and the long
Mirror which repeats the song.

For the litany of doubt
From these walls comes breathing out
Till the room becomes a pit
Humming with the fear of it

With the fear of loneliness
And uncommunicableness;
All the wires are cut, my friends
Live beyond the severed ends.

So I write these lines for you
Who have felt the death-wish too,
But your lust for life prevails –
Drinking coffee, telling tales.

Our prerogatives as men
Will be cancelled who knows when;
Still I drink your health before
The gun-butt raps upon the door.

Hidden Ice

There are few songs for domesticity
For routine work, money-making or scholarship
Though these are apt for eulogy or for tragedy.

And I would praise our adaptability
Who can spend years and years in offices and beds
Every morning twirling the napkin ring,
A twitter of inconsequent vitality.

And I would praise our inconceivable stamina
Who work to the clock and calendar and maintain
The equilibrium of nerves and notions,
Our mild bravado in the face of time.

Those who ignore disarm. The domestic ambush
The pleated lampshade the defeatist clock
May never be consummated and we may never
Strike on the rock beneath the calm upholstering.

But some though buoyed by habit, though convoyed
By habitual faces and hands that help the food
Or help one with one's coat, have lost their bearings
Struck hidden ice or currents no one noted.

One was found like Judas kissing flowers
And one who sat between the clock and the sun
Lies like a Saint Sebastian full of arrows
Feathered from his own hobby, his pet hours.

The Brandy Glass

Only let it form within his hands once more –
The moment cradled like a brandy glass.
Sitting alone in the empty dining hall . . .
From the chandeliers the snow begins to fall
Piling around carafes and table legs
And chokes the passage of the revolving door.
The last diner, like a ventriloquist's doll
Left by his master, gazes before him, begs:
'Only let it form within my hands once more.'

The Sunlight on the Garden

The sunlight on the garden
Hardens and grows cold,
We cannot cage the minute
Within its nets of gold,
When all is told
We cannot beg for pardon.

Our freedom as free lances
Advances towards its end;
The earth compels, upon it
Sonnets and birds descend;
And soon, my friend,
We shall have no time for dances.

The sky was good for flying
Defying the church bells
And every evil iron
Siren and what it tells:
The earth compels,
We are dying, Egypt, dying

And not expecting pardon,
Hardened in heart anew,
But glad to have sat under
Thunder and rain with you,
And grateful too
For sunlight on the garden.

[38]

The Hebrides

On those islands
The west wind drops its message of indolence,
No one hurries, the Gulf Stream warms the gnarled
Rampart of gneiss, the feet of the peasant years
Pad up and down their sentry-beat not challenging
Any comer for the password – only Death
Comes through unchallenged in his general's cape.
The houses straggle on the umber moors,
The Aladdin lamp mutters in the boarded room
Where a woman smoors the fire of fragrant peat.
No one repeats the password for it is known,
All is known before it comes to the lips –
Instinctive wisdom. Over the fancy vases
The photos with the wrinkles taken out,
The enlarged portraits of the successful sons
Who married wealth in Toronto or New York,
Console the lonely evenings of the old
Who live embanked by memories of labour
And child-bearing and scriptural commentaries.
On those islands
The boys go poaching their ancestral rights –
The Ossianic salmon who take the yellow
Tilt of the river with a magnet's purpose –
And listen breathless to the tales at the ceilidh
Among the peat-smoke and the smells of dung
That fill the felted room from the cave of the byre.
No window opens of the windows sunk like eyes
In a four-foot wall of stones casually picked
From the knuckly hills on which these houses crawl
Like black and legless beasts who breathe in their sleep
Among the piles of peat and pooks of hay –
A brave oasis in the indifferent moors.
And while the stories circulate like smoke,
The sense of life spreads out from the one-eyed house
In wider circles through the lake of night
In which articulate man has dropped a stone –
In wider circles round the black-faced sheep,
Wider and fainter till they hardly crease
The ebony heritage of the herded dead.

On those islands
The tinkers whom no decent girl will go with,
Preserve the Gaelic tunes unspoiled by contact
With the folk-fancier or the friendly tourist,
And preserve the knowledge of horse-flesh and preserve
The uncompromising empire of the rogue.
On those islands
The tethered cow grazes among the orchises
And figures in blue calico turn by hand
The ground beyond the plough, and the bus, not stopping,
Drops a parcel for the lonely household
Where men remembering stories of eviction
Are glad to have their land though mainly stones –
The honoured bones which still can hoist a body.
On those islands
There is echo of the leaping fish, the identical
Sound that cheered the chiefs at ease from slaughter;
There is echo of baying hounds of a lost breed
And echo of MacCrimmon's pipes lost in the cave;
And seals cry with the voices of the drowned.
When men go out to fish, no one must say 'Good luck'
And the confidences told in a boat at sea
Must be as if printed on the white ribbon of a wave
Withdrawn as soon as printed – so never heard.
On those islands
The black minister paints the tour of hell
While the unregenerate drink from the bottle's neck
In gulps like gauntlets thrown at the devil's head
And spread their traditional songs across the hills
Like fraying tapestries of fights and loves,
The boar-hunt and the rope let down at night –
Lost causes and lingering home-sickness.
On those islands
The fish come singing from the drunken sea,
The herring rush the gunwales and sort themselves
To cram the expectant barrels of their own accord –
Or such is the dream of the fisherman whose wet
Leggings hang on the door as he sleeps returned
From a night when miles of net were drawn up empty.
On those islands
A girl with candid eyes goes out to marry

An independent tenant of seven acres
Who goes each year to the south to work on the roads
In order to raise a rent of forty shillings,
And all the neighbours celebrate their wedding
With drink and pipes and the walls of the barn reflect
The crazy shadows of the whooping dancers.
On those islands
Where many live on the dole or on old-age pensions
And many waste with consumption and some are drowned
And some of the old stumble in the midst of sleep
Into the pot-hole hitherto shunned in dreams
Or falling from the cliff among the shrieks of gulls
Reach the bottom before they have time to wake –
Whoever dies on the islands and however,
The whole of the village goes into three-day mourning,
The afflicted home is honoured and the shops are shut
For on those islands
Where a few surnames cover a host of people
And the art of being a stranger with your neighbour
Has still to be imported, death is still
No lottery ticket in a public lottery –
The result to be read on the front page of a journal –
But a family matter near to the whole family.
On those islands
Where no train runs on rails and the tyrant time
Has no clock-towers to signal people to doom
With semaphore ultimatums tick by tick,
There is still peace though not for me and not
Perhaps for long – still peace on the bevel hills
For those who still can live as their fathers lived
On those islands.

Leaving Barra

The dazzle on the sea, my darling,
Leads from the western channel,
A carpet of brilliance taking
My leave for ever of the island.

I never shall visit that island
Again with its easy tempo –
The seal sunbathing, the circuit
Of gulls on the wing for garbage.

I go to a different garbage
And scuffle for scraps of notice,
Pretend to ignore the stigma
That stains my life and my leisure.

For fretful even in leisure
I fidget for different values,
Restless as a gull and haunted
By a hankering after Atlantis.

I do not know that Atlantis
Unseen and uncomprehended,
Dimly divined but keenly
Felt with a phantom hunger.

If only I could crush the hunger
If only I could lay the phantom
Then I should no doubt be happy
Like a fool or a dog or a buddha.

O the self-abnegation of Buddha
The belief that is disbelieving
The denial of chiaroscuro
Not giving a damn for existence!

But I would cherish existence
Loving the beast and the bubble
Loving the rain and the rainbow,
Considering philosophy alien.

For all the religions are alien
That allege that life is a fiction,
And when we agree in denial
The cock crows in the morning.

If only I could wake in the morning
And find I had learned the solution,
Wake with the knack of knowledge
Who as yet have only an inkling.

Though some facts foster the inkling –
The beauty of the moon and music,
The routine courage of the worker,
The gay endurance of women,

And you who to me among women
Stand for so much that I wish for,
I thank you, my dear, for the example
Of living like a fugue and moving.

For few are able to keep moving,
They drag and flag in the traffic;
While you are alive beyond question
Like the dazzle on the sea, my darling.

Chess

At the penultimate move, their saga nearly sung,
They have worked so hard to prove what lads they were when
young,
Have looked up every word in order to be able to say
The gay address unheard when they were dumb and gay.
Your Castle to King's Fourth under your practised hand!
What is the practice worth, so few being left to stand?
Better the raw levies jostling in the square
Than two old men in a crevice sniping at empty air;
The veterans on the pavement puff their cheeks and blow
The music of enslavement that echoes back 'I told you so';
The chapped hands fumble flutes, the tattered posters cry
Their craving for recruits who have not had time to die.
While our armies differ they move and feel the sun,
The victor is a cipher once the war is won.
Choose your gambit, vary the tactics of your game,
You move in a closed ambit that always ends the same.

Bagpipe Music

It's no go the merrygoround, it's no go the rickshaw,
All we want is a limousine and a ticket for the peepshow.
Their knickers are made of crêpe-de-chine, their shoes are made of
python,
Their halls are lined with tiger rugs and their walls with heads of
bison.

John MacDonald found a corpse, put it under the sofa,
Waited till it came to life and hit it with a poker,
Sold its eyes for souvenirs, sold its blood for whisky,
Kept its bones for dumb-bells to use when he was fifty.

It's no go the Yogi-Man, it's no go Blavatsky,
All we want is a bank balance and a bit of skirt in a taxi.

Annie MacDougall went to milk, caught her foot in the heather,
Woke to hear a dance record playing of Old Vienna.
It's no go your maidenheads, it's no go your culture,
All we want is a Dunlop tyre and the devil mend the puncture.

The Laird o' Phelps spent Hogmanay declaring he was sober,
Counted his feet to prove the fact and found he had one foot over.
Mrs Carmichael had her fifth, looked at the job with repulsion,
Said to the midwife 'Take it away; I'm through with over-
                                                    production.'

It's no go the gossip column, it's no go the ceilidh,
All we want is a mother's help and a sugar-stick for the baby.

Willie Murray cut his thumb, couldn't count the damage,
Took the hide of an Ayrshire cow and used it for a bandage.
His brother caught three hundred cran when the seas were lavish,
Threw the bleeders back in the sea and went upon the parish.

It's no go the Herring Board, it's no go the Bible,
All we want is a packet of fags when our hands are idle.

It's no go the picture palace, it's no go the stadium,
It's no go the country cot with a pot of pink geraniums,
It's no go the Government grants, it's no go the elections,
Sit on your arse for fifty years and hang your hat on a pension.

It's no go my honey love, it's no go my poppet;
Work your hands from day to day, the winds will blow the profit.
The glass is falling hour by hour, the glass will fall for ever,
But if you break the bloody glass you won't hold up the weather.

from Autumn Journal

Close and slow, summer is ending in Hampshire,
    Ebbing away down ramps of shaven lawn where close-clipped
                                 yew
Insulates the lives of retired generals and admirals
    And the spyglasses hung in the hall and the prayer-books ready in
                                the pew
And August going out to the tin trumpets of nasturtiums
    And the sunflowers' Salvation Army blare of brass
And the spinster sitting in a deckchair picking up stitches
    Not raising her eyes to the noise of the planes that pass
Northward from Lee-on-Solent. Macrocarpa and cypress
    And roses on a rustic trellis and mulberry trees
And bacon and eggs in a silver dish for breakfast
    And all the inherited assets of bodily ease
And all the inherited worries, rheumatism and taxes,
    And whether Stella will marry and what to do with Dick
And the branch of the family that lost their money in Hatry
    And the passing of the *Morning Post* and of life's climacteric
And the growth of vulgarity, cars that pass the gate-lodge
    And crowds undressing on the beach
And the hiking cockney lovers with thoughts directed
    Neither to God nor Nation but each to each.
But the home is still a sanctum under the pelmets,
    All quiet on the Family Front,
Farmyard noises across the fields at evening
    While the trucks of the Southern Railway dawdle . . . shunt
Into poppy sidings for the night – night which knows no passion
    No assault of hands or tongue
For all is old as flint or chalk or pine-needles
    And the rebels and the young
Have taken the train to town or the two-seater
    Unravelling rails or road,
Losing the thread deliberately behind them –
    Autumnal palinode.
And I am in the train too now and summer is going
    South as I go north
Bound for the dead leaves falling, the burning bonfire,

The dying that brings forth
The harder life, revealing the trees' girders,
    The frost that kills the germs of *laissez-faire*;
West Meon, Tisted, Farnham, Woking, Weybridge,
    Then London's packed and stale and pregnant air.
My dog, a symbol of the abandoned order,
    Lies on the carriage floor,
Her eyes inept and glamorous as a film star's,
    Who wants to live, i.e. wants more
Presents, jewellery, furs, gadgets, solicitations
    As if to live were not
Following the curve of a planet or controlled water
    But a leap in the dark, a tangent, a stray shot.
It is this we learn after so many failures,
    The building of castles in sand, of queens in snow,
That we cannot make any corner in life or in life's beauty,
    That no river is a river which does not flow.
Surbiton, and a woman gets in, painted
    With dyed hair but a ladder in her stocking and eyes
Patient beneath the calculated lashes,
    Inured for ever to surprise;
And the train's rhythm becomes the *ad nauseam* repetition
    Of every tired aubade and maudlin madrigal,
The faded airs of sexual attraction
    Wandering like dead leaves along a warehouse wall:
'I loved my love with a platform ticket,
    A jazz song,
A handbag, a pair of stockings of Paris Sand –
    I loved her long.
I loved her between the lines and against the clock,
    Not until death
But till life did us part I loved her with paper money
    And with whisky on the breath.
I loved her with peacock's eyes and the wares of Carthage,
    With glass and gloves and gold and a powder puff
With blasphemy, camaraderie, and bravado
    And lots of other stuff.
I loved my love with the wings of angels
    Dipped in henna, unearthly red,
With my office hours, with flowers and sirens,
    With my budget, my latchkey, and my daily bread.'

And so to London and down the ever-moving
  Stairs
Where a warm wind blows the bodies of men together
  And blows apart their complexes and cares.

IV

September has come and I wake
  And I think with joy how whatever, now or in future, the system
Nothing whatever can take
  The people away, there will always be people
For friends or for lovers though perhaps
  The conditions of love will be changed and its vices diminished
And affection not lapse
  To narrow possessiveness, jealousy founded on vanity.
September has come, it is *hers*
  Whose vitality leaps in the autumn,
Whose nature prefers
  Trees without leaves and a fire in the fireplace;
So I give her this month and the next
  Though the whole of my year should be hers who has rendered
                                                      already
So many of its days intolerable or perplexed
  But so many more so happy;
Who has left a scent on my life and left my walls
  Dancing over and over with her shadow,
Whose hair is twined in all my waterfalls
  And all of London littered with remembered kisses.
So I am glad
  That life contains her with her moods and moments
More shifting and more transient than I had
  Yet thought of as being integral to beauty;
Whose mind is like the wind on a sea of wheat,
  Whose eyes are candour,
And assurance in her feet
  Like a homing pigeon never by doubt diverted.
To whom I send my thanks
  That the air has become shot silk, the streets are music,
And that the ranks
  Of men are ranks of men, no more of ciphers.
So that if now alone

[48]

I must pursue this life, it will not be only
A drag from numbered stone to numbered stone
    But a ladder of angels, river turning tidal.
Off-hand, at times hysterical, abrupt,
    You are one I always shall remember,
Whom cant can never corrupt
    Nor argument disinherit.
Frivolous, always in a hurry, forgetting the address,
    Frowning too often, taking enormous notice
Of hats and backchat – how could I assess
    The thing that makes you different?
You whom I remember glad or tired,
    Smiling in drink or scintillating anger,
Inopportunely desired
    On boats, on trains, on roads when walking.
Sometimes untidy, often elegant,
    So easily hurt, so readily responsive,
To whom a trifle could be an irritant
    Or could be balm and manna.
Whose words would tumble over each other and pelt
    From pure excitement,
Whose fingers curl and melt
    When you were friendly.
I shall remember you in bed with bright
    Eyes or in a café stirring coffee
Abstractedly and on your plate the white
    Smoking stub your lips had touched with crimson.
And I shall remember how your words could hurt
    Because they were so honest
And even your lies were able to assert
    Integrity of purpose.
And it is on the strength of knowing you
    I reckon generous feeling more important
Than the mere deliberating what to do
    When neither the pros nor cons affect the pulses.
And though I have suffered from your special strength
    Who never flatter for points nor fake responses
I should be proud if I could evolve at length
    An equal thrust and pattern.

[49]

And I remember Spain
  At Easter ripe as an egg for revolt and ruin
Though for a tripper the rain
  Was worse than the surly or the worried or the haunted faces
With writings on the walls –
  Hammer and sickle, Boicot, Viva, Muerra;
With café-au-lait brimming the waterfalls,
  With sherry, shellfish, omelettes.
With fretted stone the Moor
  Had chiselled for effects of sun and shadow;
With shadows of the poor,
  The begging cripples and the children begging.
The churches full of saints
  Tortured on racks of marble –
The old complaints
  Covered with gilt and dimly lit with candles.
With powerful or banal
  Monuments of riches or repression
And the Escorial
  Cold for ever within like the heart of Philip.
With ranks of dominoes
  Deployed on café tables the whole of Sunday;
With cabarets that call the tourist, shows
  Of thighs and eyes and nipples.
With slovenly soldiers, nuns,
  And peeling posters from the last elections
Promising bread or guns
  Or an amnesty or another
Order or else the old
  Glory veneered and varnished
As if veneer could hold
  The rotten guts and crumbled bones together.
And a vulture hung in air
  Below the cliffs of Ronda and below him
His hook-winged shadow wavered like despair
  Across the chequered vineyards.
And the boot-blacks in Madrid
  Kept us half an hour with polish and pincers

And all we did
  In that city was drink and think and loiter.
And in the Prado half-
  wit princes looked from the canvas they had paid for
(Goya had the laugh –
  But can what is corrupt be cured by laughter?)
And the day at Aranjuez
  When the sun came out for once on the yellow river
With Valdepeñas burdening the breath
  We slept a royal sleep in the royal gardens;
And at Toledo walked
  Around the ramparts where they throw the garbage
And glibly talked
  Of how the Spaniards lack all sense of business.
And Avila was cold
  And Segovia was picturesque and smelly
And a goat on the road seemed old
  As the rocks or the Roman arches.
And Easter was wet and full
  In Seville and in the ring on Easter Sunday
A clumsy bull and then a clumsy bull
  Nodding his banderillas died of boredom.
And the standard of living was low
  But that, we thought to ourselves, was not our business;
All that the tripper wants is the *status quo*
  Cut and dried for trippers.
And we thought the papers a lark
  With their party politics and blank invective;
And we thought the dark
    Women who dyed their hair should have it dyed more often.
And we sat in trains all night
  With the windows shut among civil guards and peasants
And tried to play piquet by a tiny light
  And tried to sleep bolt upright;
And cursed the Spanish rain
  And cursed their cigarettes which came to pieces
And caught heavy colds in Cordova and in vain
  Waited for the right light for taking photos.
And we met a Cambridge don who said with an air

'There's going to be trouble shortly in this country,'
And ordered anis, pudgy and debonair,
  Glad to show off his mastery of the language.
But only an inch behind
  This map of olive and ilex, this painted hoarding,
Careless of visitors the people's mind
  Was tunnelling like a mole to day and danger.
And the day before we left
  We saw the mob in flower at Algeciras
Outside a toothless door, a church bereft
  Of its images and its aura.
And at La Linea while
  The night put miles between us and Gibraltar
We heard the blood-lust of a drunkard pile
  His heaven high with curses;
And next day took the boat
  For home, forgetting Spain, not realizing
That Spain would soon denote
  Our grief, our aspirations;
Not knowing that our blunt
  Ideals would find their whetstone, that our spirit
Would find its frontier on the Spanish front,
  Its body in a rag-tag army.

VII

Conferences, adjournments, ultimatums,
  Flights in the air, castles in the air,
The autopsy of treaties, dynamite under the bridges,
  The end of *laissez-faire*.
After the warm days the rain comes pimpling
  The paving stones with white
And with the rain the national conscience, creeping,
  Seeping through the night.
And in the sodden park on Sunday protest
  Meetings assemble not, as so often, now
Merely to advertise some patent panacea
  But simply to avow
The need to hold the ditch; a bare avowal
  That may perhaps imply
Death at the doors in a week but perhaps in the long run

Exposure of the lie.
Think of a number, double it, treble it, square it,
  And sponge it out
And repeat *ad lib.* and mark the slate with crosses;
  There is no time to doubt
If the puzzle really has an answer. Hitler yells on the wireless,
  The night is damp and still
And I hear dull blows on wood outside my window;
  They are cutting down the trees on Primrose Hill.
The wood is white like the roast flesh of chicken,
  Each tree falling like a closing fan;
No more looking at the view from seats beneath the branches,
  Everything is going to plan;
They want the crest of this hill for anti-aircraft,
  The guns will take the view
And searchlights probe the heavens for bacilli
  With narrow wands of blue.
And the rain came on as I watched the territorials
  Sawing and chopping and pulling on ropes like a team
In a village tug-of-war; and I found my dog had vanished
  And thought 'This is the end of the old regime,'
But found the police had got her at St John's Wood station
  And fetched her in the rain and went for a cup
Of coffee to an all-night shelter and heard a taxi-driver
  Say 'It turns me up
When I see these soldiers in lorries' – rumble of tumbrils
  Drums in the trees
Breaking the eardrums of the ravished dryads –
  It turns me up; a coffee, please.
And as I go out I see a windscreen-wiper
  In an empty car
Wiping away like mad and I feel astounded
  That things have gone so far.
And I come back here to my flat and wonder whether
  From now on I need take
The trouble to go out choosing stuff for curtains
  As I don't know anyone to make
Curtains quickly. Rather one should quickly
  Stop the cracks for gas or dig a trench
And take one's paltry measures against the coming
  Of the unknown Uebermensch.

But one – meaning I – is bored, am bored, the issue
 Involving principle but bound in fact
To squander principle in panic and self-deception –
 Accessories after the act,
So that all we foresee is rivers in spate sprouting
 With drowning hands
And men like dead frogs floating till the rivers
 Lose themselves in the sands.
And we who have been brought up to think of 'Gallant Belgium'
 As so much blague
Are now preparing again to essay good through evil
 For the sake of Prague;
And must, we suppose, become uncritical, vindictive,
 And must, in order to beat
The enemy, model ourselves upon the enemy,
 A howling radio for our paraclete.
The night continues wet, the axe keeps falling,
 The hill grows bald and bleak
No longer one of the sights of London but maybe
 We shall have fireworks here by this day week.

VIII

Sun shines easy, sun shines gay
 On bug-house, warehouse, brewery, market,
On the chocolate factory and the BSA,
 On the Greek town hall and Josiah Mason;
On the Mitchells and Butlers Tudor pubs,
 On the white police and the one-way traffic
And glances off the chromium hubs
 And the metal studs in the sleek macadam.
Eight years back about this time
 I came to live in this hazy city
To work in a building caked with grime
 Teaching the classics to Midland students;
Virgil, Livy, the usual round,
 Principal parts and the lost digamma;
And to hear the prison-like lecture room resound
 To Homer in a Dudley accent.
But Life was comfortable, life was fine
 With two in a bed and patchwork cushions

And checks and tassels on the washing-line,
   A gramophone, a cat, and the smell of jasmine.
The steaks were tender, the films were fun,
   The walls were striped like a Russian ballet,
There were lots of things undone
   But nobody cared, for the days were early.
Nobody niggled, nobody cared,
   The soul was deaf to the mounting debit,
The soul was unprepared
   But the firelight danced on the ply-wood ceiling.
We drove round Shropshire in a bijou car –
   Bewdley, Cleobury Mortimer, Ludlow –
And the map of England was a toy bazaar
   And the telephone wires were idle music.
And sun shone easy, sun shone hard
   On quickly dropping pear-tree blossom
And pigeons courting in the cobbled yard
   With flashing necks and notes of thunder.
We slept in linen, we cooked with wine,
   We paid in cash and took no notice
Of how the train ran down the line
   Into the sun against the signal.
We lived in Birmingham through the slump –
   Line your boots with a piece of paper –
Sunlight dancing on the rubbish dump,
   On the queues of men and the hungry chimneys.
And the next election came –
   Labour defeats in Erdington and Aston;
And life went on – for us went on the same;
   Who were we to count the losses?
Some went back to work and the void
   Took on shape while others climbing
The uphill nights of the unemployed
   Woke in the morning to factory hooters.
Little on the plate and nothing in the post;
   Queue in the rain or try the public
Library where the eye may coast
   Columns of print for a hopeful harbour.
But roads ran easy, roads ran gay
   Clear of the city and we together
Could put on tweeds for a getaway

[55]

South or west to Clee or the Cotswolds;
Forty to the gallon; into the green
    Fields in the past of English history;
Flies in the bonnet and dust on the screen
    And no look back to the burning city.
That was then and now is now,
    Here again on a passing visit,
Passing through but how
    Memory blocks the passage.
Just as in Nineteen-Thirty-One
    Sun shines easy but I no longer
Docket a place in the sun –
    No wife, no ivory tower, no funk-hole.
The night grows purple, the crisis hangs
    Over the roofs like a Persian army
And all of Xenophon's parasangs
    Would take us only an inch from danger.
Black-out practice and ARP,
    Newsboys driving a roaring business,
The flapping paper snatched to see
    If anything has, or has not, happened.
And I go to the Birmingham Hippodrome
    Packed to the roof and primed for laughter
And beautifully at home
    With the ukulele and the comic chestnuts;
'As pals we meet, as pals we part' –
    Embonpoint and a new tiara;
The comedian spilling the apple-cart
    Of *doubles entendres* and doggerel verses
And the next day begins
    Again with alarm and anxious
Listening to bulletins
    From distant, measured voices
Arguing for peace
    While the zero hour approaches,
While the eagles gather and the petrol and oil and grease
    Have all been applied and the vultures back the eagles.
But once again
    The crisis is put off and things look better
And we feel negotiation is not vain –
    Save my skin and damn my conscience.

And negotiation wins,
    If you can call it winning,
And here we are – just as before – safe in our skins;
    Glory to God for Munich.
And stocks go up and wrecks
    Are salved and politicians' reputations
Go up like Jack-on-the-Beanstalk; only the Czechs
    Go down and without fighting.

IX

Now we are back to normal, now the mind is
    Back to the even tenor of the usual day
Skidding no longer across the uneasy camber
    Of the nightmare way.
We are safe though others have crashed the railings
    Over the river ravine; their wheel-tracks carve the bank
But after the event all we can do is argue
    And count the widening ripples where they sank.
October comes with rain whipping around the ankles
    In waves of white at night
And filling the raw clay trenches (the parks of London
    Are a nasty sight).
In a week I return to work, lecturing, coaching,
    As impresario of the Ancient Greeks
Who wore the chiton and lived on fish and olives
    And talked philosophy or smut in cliques;
Who believed in youth and did not gloze the unpleasant
    Consequences of age;
What is life, one said, or what is pleasant
    Once you have turned the page
Of love? The days grow worse, the dice are loaded
    Against the living man who pays in tears for breath;
Never to be born was the best, call no man happy
    This side death.
Conscious – long before Engels – of necessity
    And therein free
They plotted out their life with truism and humour
    Between the jealous heaven and the callous sea.
And Pindar sang the garland of wild olive
    And Alcibiades lived from hand to mouth

Double-crossing Athens, Persia, Sparta,
    And many died in the city of plague, and many of drouth
In Sicilian quarries, and many by the spear and arrow
    And many more who told their lies too late
Caught in the eternal factions and reactions
    Of the city-state.
And free speech shivered on the pikes of Macedonia
    And later on the swords of Rome
And Athens became a mere university city
    And the goddess born of the foam
Became the kept hetaera, heroine of Menander,
    And the philosopher narrowed his focus, confined
His efforts to putting his own soul in order
    And keeping a quiet mind.
And for a thousand years they went on talking,
    Making such apt remarks,
A race no longer of heroes but of professors
    And crooked business men and secretaries and clerks
Who turned out dapper little elegiac verses
    On the ironies of fate, the transience of all
Affections, carefully shunning an over-statement
    But working the dying fall.
The Glory that was Greece: put it in a syllabus, grade it
    Page by page
To train the mind or even to point a moral
    For the present age:
Models of logic and lucidity, dignity, sanity,
    The golden mean between opposing ills
Though there were exceptions of course but only exceptions –
    The bloody Bacchanals on the Thracian hills.
So the humanist in his room with Jacobean panels
    Chewing his pipe and looking on a lazy quad
Chops the Ancient World to turn a sermon
    To the greater glory of God.
But I can do nothing so useful or so simple;
    These dead are dead
And when I should remember the paragons of Hellas
    I think instead
Of the crooks, the adventurers, the opportunists,
    The careless athletes and the fancy boys,
The hair-splitters, the pedants, the hard-boiled sceptics

And the Agora and the noise
Of the demagogues and the quacks; and the women pouring
    Libations over graves
And the trimmers at Delphi and the dummies at Sparta and lastly
    I think of the slaves.
And how one can imagine oneself among them
    I do not know;
It was all so unimaginably different
    And all so long ago.

xv

Shelley and jazz and lieder and love and hymn-tunes
    And day returns too soon;
We'll get drunk among the roses
    In the valley of the moon.
Give me an aphrodisiac, give me lotus,
    Give me the same again;
Make all the erotic poets of Rome and Ionia
    And Florence and Provence and Spain
Pay a tithe of their sugar to my potion
    And ferment my days
With the twang of Hawaii and the boom of the Congo,
    Let the old Muse loosen her stays
Or give me a new Muse with stockings and suspenders
    And a smile like a cat,
With false eyelashes and finger-nails of carmine
    And dressed by Schiaparelli, with a pill-box hat.
Let the aces run riot round Brooklands,
    Let the tape-machines go drunk,
Turn on the purple spotlight, pull out the Vox Humana,
    Dig up somebody's body in a cloakroom trunk.
Give us sensations and then again sensations –
    Strip-tease, fireworks, all-in wrestling, gin;
Spend your capital, open your house and pawn your padlocks,
    Let the critical sense go out and the Roaring Boys come in.
Give me a houri but houris are too easy,
    Give me a nun;
We'll rape the angels off the golden reredos
    Before we're done.
Tiger-women and Lesbos, drums and entrails,

[59]

And let the skies rotate,
We'll play roulette with the stars, we'll sit out drinking
    At the Hangman's Gate.
O look who comes here. I cannot see their faces
    Walking in file, slowly in file;
They have no shoes on their feet, the knobs of their ankles
    Catch the moonlight as they pass the stile
And cross the moor among the skeletons of bog-oak
    Following the track from the gallows back to the town;
Each has the end of a rope around his neck. I wonder
    Who let these men come back, who cut them down –
And now they reach the gate and line up opposite
    The neon lights on the medieval wall
And underneath the sky-signs
    Each one takes his cowl and lets it fall
And we see their faces, each the same as the other,
    Men and women, each like a closed door,
But something about their faces is familiar;
    Where have we seen them before?
Was it the murderer on the nursery ceiling
    Or Judas Iscariot in the Field of Blood
Or someone at Gallipoli or in Flanders
    Caught in the end-all mud?
But take no notice of them, out with the ukulele,
    The saxophone and the dice;
They are sure to go away if we take no notice;
    Another round of drinks or make it twice.
That was a good one, tell us another, don't stop talking,
    Cap your stories; if
You haven't any new ones tell the old ones,
    Tell them as often as you like and perhaps those horrible stiff
People with blank faces that are yet familiar
    Won't be there when you look again, but don't
Look just yet, just give them time to vanish. I said to vanish;
    What do you mean – they won't?
Give us the songs of Harlem or Mitylene –
    Pearls in wine –
There can't be a hell unless there is a heaven
    And a devil would have to be divine
And there can't be such things one way or the other;
    That we know;

You can't step into the same river twice so there can't be
    Ghosts; thank God that rivers always flow.
Sufficient to the moment is the moment;
    Past and future merely don't make sense
And yet I thought I had seen them . . .
    But *how*, if there is only a present tense?
Come on, boys, we aren't afraid of bogies,
    Give us another drink;
This little lady has a fetish,
    She goes to bed in mink.
This little pig went to market –
    Now I think you may look, I think the coast is clear.
Well, why don't you answer?
    I can't answer because they are still there.

XVI

Nightmare leaves fatigue:
    We envy men of action
Who sleep and wake, murder and intrigue
    Without being doubtful, without being haunted.
And I envy the intransigence of my own
    Countrymen who shoot to kill and never
See the victim's face become their own
    Or find his motive sabotage their motives.
So reading the memoirs of Maud Gonne,
    Daughter of an English mother and a soldier father,
I note how a single purpose can be founded on
    A jumble of opposites:
Dublin Castle, the vice-regal ball,
    The embassies of Europe,
Hatred scribbled on a wall,
    Gaols and revolvers.
And I remember, when I was little, the fear
    Bandied among the servants
That Casement would land at the pier
    With a sword and a horde of rebels;
And how we used to expect, at a later date,
    When the wind blew from the west, the noise of shooting
Starting in the evening at eight
    In Belfast in the York Street district;

And the voodoo of the Orange bands
    Drawing an iron net through darkest Ulster,
Flailing the limbo lands –
    The linen mills, the long wet grass, the ragged hawthorn.
And one read black where the other read white, his hope
    The other man's damnation:
Up the Rebels, To Hell with the Pope,
    And God Save – as you prefer – the King or Ireland.
The land of scholars and saints:
    Scholars and saints my eye, the land of ambush,
Purblind manifestoes, never-ending complaints,
    The born martyr and the gallant ninny;
The grocer drunk with the drum,
    The land-owner shot in his bed, the angry voices
Piercing the broken fanlight in the slum,
    The shawled woman weeping at the garish altar.
Kathaleen ni Houlihan! Why
    Must a country, like a ship or a car, be always female,
Mother or sweetheart? A woman passing by,
    We did but see her passing.
Passing like a patch of sun on the rainy hill
    And yet we love her for ever and hate our neighbour
And each one in his will
    Binds his heirs to continuance of hatred.
Drums on the haycock, drums on the harvest, black
    Drums in the night shaking the windows:
King William is riding his white horse back
    To the Boyne on a banner.
Thousands of banners, thousands of white
    Horses, thousands of Williams
Waving thousands of swords and ready to fight
    Till the blue sea turns to orange.
Such was my country and I thought I was well
    Out of it, educated and domiciled in England,
Though yet her name keeps ringing like a bell
    In an under-water belfry.
Why do we like being Irish? Partly because
    It gives us a hold on the sentimental English
As members of a world that never was,
    Baptized with fairy water;
And partly because Ireland is small enough

To be still thought of with a family feeling,
And because the waves are rough
   That split her from a more commercial culture;
And because one feels that here at least one can
   Do local work which is not at the world's mercy
And that on this tiny stage with luck a man
   Might see the end of one particular action.
It is self-deception of course;
   There is no immunity in this island either;
A cart that is drawn by somebody else's horse
   And carrying goods to somebody else's market.
The bombs in the turnip sack, the sniper from the roof,
   Griffith, Connolly, Collins, where have they brought us?
Ourselves alone! Let the round tower stand aloof
   In a world of bursting mortar!
Let the school-children fumble their sums
   In a half-dead language;
Let the censor be busy on the books; pull down the Georgian slums;
   Let the games be played in Gaelic.
Let them grow beet-sugar; let them build
   A factory in every hamlet;
Let them pigeon-hole the souls of the killed
   Into sheep and goats, patriots and traitors.
And the North, where I was a boy,
   Is still the North, veneered with the grime of Glasgow,
Thousands of men whom nobody will employ
   Standing at the corners, coughing.
And the street-children play on the wet
   Pavement – hopscotch or marbles;
And each rich family boasts a sagging tennis-net
   On a spongy lawn beside a dripping shrubbery.
The smoking chimneys hint
   At prosperity round the corner
But they make their Ulster linen from foreign lint
   And the money that comes in goes out to make more money.
A city built upon mud;
   A culture built upon profit,
Free speech nipped in the bud,
   The minority always guilty.
Why should I want to go back
   To you, Ireland, my Ireland?

The blots on the page are so black
    That they cannot be covered with shamrock.
I hate your grandiose airs,
    Your sob-stuff, your laugh and your swagger,
Your assumption that everyone cares
    Who is the king of your castle.
Castles are out of date,
    The tide flows round the children's sandy fancy;
Put up what flag you like, it is too late
    To save your soul with bunting.
Odi atque amo:
    Shall we cut this name on trees with a rusty dagger?
Her mountains are still blue, her rivers flow
    Bubbling over the boulders.
She is both a bore and a bitch;
    Better close the horizon,
Send her no more fantasy, no more longings which
    Are under a fatal tariff.
For common sense is the vogue
    And she gives her children neither sense nor money
Who slouch around the world with a gesture and a brogue
    And a faggot of useless memories.

from xx

A week to Christmas, cards of snow and holly,
    Gimcracks in the shops,
Wishes and memories wrapped in tissue paper,
    Trinkets, gadgets and lollipops
And as if through coloured glasses
    We remember our childhood's thrill
Waking in the morning to the rustling of paper,
    The eiderdown heaped in a hill
Of wogs and dogs and bears and bricks and apples
    And the feeling that Christmas Day
Was a coral island in time where we land and eat our lotus
    But where we can never stay.
There was a star in the East, the magi in their turbans
    Brought their luxury toys
In homage to a child born to capsize their values
    And wreck their equipoise.

A smell of hay like peace in the dark stable –
  Not peace however but a sword
To cut the Gordian knot of logical self-interest,
  The fool-proof golden cord;
For Christ walked in where no philosopher treads
  But armed with more than folly,
Making the smooth place rough and knocking the heads
  Of Church and State together.
In honour of whom we have taken over the pagan
  Saturnalia for our annual treat
Letting the belly have its say, ignoring
  The spirit while we eat.
And Conscience still goes crying through the desert
  With sackcloth round his loins:
A week to Christmas – hark the herald angels
  Beg for copper coins.

XXIV

Sleep, my body, sleep, my ghost,
  Sleep, my parents and grand-parents,
And all those I have loved most:
  One man's coffin is another's cradle.
Sleep, my past and all my sins,
  In distant snow or dried roses
Under the moon for night's cocoon will open
  When day begins.
Sleep, my fathers, in your graves
  On upland bogland under heather;
What the wind scatters the wind saves,
  A sapling springs in a new country.
Time is a country, the present moment
  A spotlight roving round the scene;
We need not chase the spotlight,
  The future is the bride of what has been.
Sleep, my fancies and my wishes,
  Sleep a little and wake strong,
The same but different and take my blessing –
  A cradle-song.
And sleep, my various and conflicting
  Selves I have so long endured,

Sleep in Asclepius' temple
  And wake cured.
And you with whom I shared an idyll
  Five years long,
Sleep beyond the Atlantic
  And wake to a glitter of dew and to bird-song.
And you whose eyes are blue, whose ways are foam,
  Sleep quiet and smiling
And do not hanker
  For a perfection which can never come.
And you whose minutes patter
  To crowd the social hours,
Curl up easy in a placid corner
  And let your thoughts close in like flowers.
And you, who work for Christ, and you, as eager
  For a better life, humanist, atheist,
And you, devoted to a cause, and you, to a family,
  Sleep and may your beliefs and zeal persist.
Sleep quietly, Marx and Freud,
  The figure-heads of our transition.
Cagney, Lombard, Bing and Garbo,
  Sleep in your world of celluloid.
Sleep now also, monk and satyr,
  Cease your wrangling for a night.
Sleep, my brain, and sleep, my senses,
  Sleep, my hunger and my spite.
Sleep, recruits to the evil army,
  Who, for so long misunderstood,
Took to the gun to kill your sorrow;
  Sleep and be damned and wake up good.
While we sleep, what shall we dream?
  Of Tir nan Og or South Sea islands,
Of a land where all the milk is cream
  And all the girls are willing?
Or shall our dream be earnest of the real
  Future when we wake,
Design a home, a factory, a fortress
  Which, though with effort, we can really make?
What is it we want really?
  For what end and how?
If it is something feasible, obtainable,

Let us dream it now,
And pray for a possible land
   Not of sleep-walkers, not of angry puppets,
But where both heart and brain can understand
   The movements of our fellows;
Where life is a choice of instruments and none
   Is debarred his natural music,
Where the waters of life are free of the ice-blockade of hunger
   And thought is free as the sun,
Where the altars of sheer power and mere profit
   Have fallen to disuse,
Where nobody sees the use
   Of buying money and blood at the cost of blood and money,
Where the individual, no longer squandered
   In self-assertion, works with the rest, endowed
With the split vision of a juggler and the quick lock of a taxi,
   Where the people are more than a crowd.
So sleep in hope of this – but only for a little;
   Your hope must wake
While the choice is yours to make,
   The mortgage not foreclosed, the offer open.
Sleep serene, avoid the backward
   Glance; go forward, dreams, and do not halt
(Behind you in the desert stands a token
   Of doubt – a pillar of salt).
Sleep, the past, and wake, the future,
   And walk out promptly through the open door;
But you, my coward doubts, may go on sleeping,
   You need not wake again – not any more.
The New Year comes with bombs, it is too late
   To dose the dead with honourable intentions:
If you have honour to spare, employ it on the living;
   The dead are dead as Nineteen-Thirty-Eight.
Sleep to the noise of running water
   Tomorrow to be crossed, however deep;
This is no river of the dead or Lethe,
   Tonight we sleep
On the banks of Rubicon – the die is cast;
   There will be time to audit
The accounts later, there will be sunlight later
   And the equation will come out at last.

Prognosis

Goodbye, Winter,
The days are getting longer,
The tea-leaf in the teacup
Is herald of a stranger.

Will he bring me business
Or will he bring me gladness
Or will he come for cure
Of his own sickness?

With a pedlar's burden
Walking up the garden
Will he come to beg
Or will he come to bargain?

Will he come to pester,
To cringe or to bluster,
A promise in his palm
Or a gun in his holster?

Will his name be John
Or will his name be Jonah
Crying to repent
On the Island of Iona?

Will his name be Jason
Looking for a seaman
Or a mad crusader
Without rhyme or reason?

What will be his message –
War or work or marriage?
News as new as dawn
Or an old adage?

Will he give a champion
Answer to my question
Or will his words be dark
And his ways evasion?

Will his name be Love
And all his talk be crazy?
Or will his name be Death
And his message easy?

Stylite

The saint on the pillar stands,
The pillar is alone,
He has stood so long
That he himself is stone;
Only his eyes
Range across the sand
Where no one ever comes
And the world is banned.

Then his eyes close,
He stands in his sleep,
Round his neck there comes
The conscience of a rope,
And the hangman counting
Counting to ten –
At nine he finds
He has eyes again.

The saint on the pillar stands,
The pillars are two,
A young man opposite
Stands in the blue,
A white Greek god,
Confident, with curled
Hair above the groin
And his eyes on the world.

Entirely

If we could get the hang of it entirely
  It would take too long;
All we know is the splash of words in passing
  And falling twigs of song,
And when we try to eavesdrop on the great
  Presences it is rarely
That by a stroke of luck we can appropriate
  Even a phrase entirely.

If we could find our happiness entirely
  In somebody else's arms
We should not fear the spears of the spring nor the city's
  Yammering fire alarms
But, as it is, the spears each year go through
  Our flesh and almost hourly
Bell or siren banishes the blue
  Eyes of Love entirely.

And if the world were black or white entirely
  And all the charts were plain
Instead of a mad weir of tigerish waters,
  A prism of delight and pain,
We might be surer where we wished to go
  Or again we might be merely
Bored but in brute reality there is no
  Road that is right entirely.

London Rain

The rain of London pimples
The ebony street with white
And the neon-lamps of London
Stain the canals of night
And the park becomes a jungle
In the alchemy of night.

My wishes turn to violent
Horses black as coal –
The randy mares of fancy,
The stallions of the soul –
Eager to take the fences
That fence about my soul.

Across the countless chimneys
The horses ride and across
The country to the channel
Where warning beacons toss,
To a place where God and No-God
Play at pitch and toss.

Whichever wins I am happy
For God will give me bliss
But No-God will absolve me
From all I do amiss
And I need not suffer conscience
If the world was made amiss.

Under God we can reckon
On pardon when we fall
But if we are under No-God
Nothing will matter at all,
Arson and rape and murder
Must count for nothing at all.

So reinforced by logic
As having nothing to lose
My lust goes riding horseback
To ravish where I choose,
To burgle all the turrets
Of beauty as I choose.

But now the rain gives over
Its dance upon the town,
Logic and lust together
Come dimly tumbling down,
And neither God nor No-God
Is either up or down.

The argument was wilful,
The alternatives untrue,
We need no metaphysics
To sanction what we do
Or to muffle us in comfort
From what we did not do.

Whether the living river
Began in bog or lake,
The world is what was given,
The world is what we make
And we only can discover
Life in the life we make.

So let the water sizzle
Upon the gleaming slates,
There will be sunshine after
When the rain abates
And rain returning duly
When the sun abates.

My wishes now come homeward,
Their gallopings in vain,
Logic and lust are quiet,
Once more it starts to rain.
Falling asleep I listen
To the falling London rain.

from Trilogy for X

And love hung still as crystal over the bed
    And filled the corners of the enormous room;
The boom of dawn that left her sleeping, showing
    The flowers mirrored in the mahogany table.

O my love, if only I were able
    To protract this hour of quiet after passion,
Not ration happiness but keep this door for ever
    Closed on the world, its own world closed within it.

But dawn's waves trouble with the bubbling minute,
    The names of books come clear upon their shelves,
The reason delves for duty and you will wake
    With a start and go on living on your own.

The first train passes and the windows groan,
    Voices will hector and your voice become
A drum in tune with theirs, which all last night
    Like sap that fingered through a hungry tree
Asserted our one night's identity.

The Closing Album

I

Dublin

Grey brick upon brick,
Declamatory bronze
On sombre pedestals –
O'Connell, Grattan, Moore –
And the brewery tugs and the swans
On the balustraded stream
And the bare bones of a fanlight
Over a hungry door
And the air soft on the cheek
And porter running from the taps
With a head of yellow cream
And Nelson on his pillar
Watching his world collapse.

This was never my town,
I was not born nor bred
Nor schooled here and she will not
Have me alive or dead
But yet she holds my mind
With her seedy elegance,
With her gentle veils of rain
And all her ghosts that walk
And all that hide behind
Her Georgian façades –
The catcalls and the pain,
The glamour of her squalor,
The bravado of her talk.

The lights jig in the river
With a concertina movement
And the sun comes up in the morning
Like barley-sugar on the water
And the mist on the Wicklow hills
Is close, as close
As the peasantry were to the landlord,
As the Irish to the Anglo-Irish,

As the killer is close one moment
To the man he kills,
Or as the moment itself
Is close to the next moment.

She is not an Irish town
And she is not English,
Historic with guns and vermin
And the cold renown
Of a fragment of Church Latin,
Of an oratorical phrase.
But oh the days are soft,
Soft enough to forget
The lesson better learnt,
The bullet on the wet
Streets, the crooked deal,
The steel behind the laugh,
The Four Courts burnt.

Fort of the Dane,
Garrison of the Saxon,
Augustan capital
Of a Gaelic nation,
Appropriating all
The alien brought,
You give me time for thought
And by a juggler's trick
You poise the toppling hour –
O greyness run to flower,
Grey stone, grey water,
And brick upon grey brick.

Cushendun

Fuchsia and ragweed and the distant hills
Made as it were out of clouds and sea:
All night the bay is plashing and the moon
   Marks the break of the waves.

Limestone and basalt and a whitewashed house
With passages of great stone flags
And a walled garden with plums on the wall
   And a bird piping in the night.

Forgetfulness: brass lamps and copper jugs
And home-made bread and the smell of turf or flax
And the air a glove and the water lathering easy
   And convolvulus in the hedge.

Only in the dark green room beside the fire
With the curtains drawn against the winds and waves
There is a little box with a well-bred voice:
   What a place to talk of War.

III
Sligo and Mayo

In Sligo the country was soft; there were turkeys
   Gobbling under sycamore trees
And the shadows of clouds on the mountains moving
   Like browsing cattle at ease.

And little distant fields were sprigged with haycocks
   And splashed against a white
Roadside cottage a welter of nasturtium
   Deluging the sight,

And pullets pecking the flies from around the eyes of heifers
   Sitting in farmyard mud
Among hydrangeas and the falling ear-rings
   Of fuchsias red as blood.

But in Mayo the tumbledown walls went leap-frog
  Over the moors,
The sugar and salt in the pubs were damp in the casters
  And the water was brown as beer upon the shores

Of desolate loughs, and stumps of hoary bog-oak
  Stuck up here and there
And as the twilight filtered on the heather
  Water-music filled the air,

And when the night came down upon the bogland
  With all-enveloping wings
The coal-black turf-stacks rose against the darkness
  Like the tombs of nameless kings.

IV

Galway

O the crossbones of Galway,
The hollow grey houses,
The rubbish and sewage,
The grass-grown pier,
And the dredger grumbling
All night in the harbour:
The war came down on us here.

Salmon in the Corrib
Gently swaying
And the water combed out
Over the weir
And a hundred swans
Dreaming on the harbour:
The war came down on us here.

The night was gay
With the moon's music
But Mars was angry
On the hills of Clare
And September dawned
Upon willows and ruins:
The war came down on us here.

Why, now it has happened,
Should the clock go on striking to the firedogs
And why should the rooks be blown upon the evening
Like burnt paper in a chimney?

And why should the sea maintain its turbulence, its elegance,
And draw a film of muslin down the sand
With each receding wave?

And why, now it has happened,
Should the atlas still be full of the maps of countries
We never shall see again?

And why, now it has happened,
And doom all night is lapping at the door,
Should I remember that I ever met you –
Once in another world?

August–September 1939

Meeting Point

Time was away and somewhere else,
There were two glasses and two chairs
And two people with the one pulse
(Somebody stopped the moving stairs):
Time was away and somewhere else.

And they were neither up nor down;
The stream's music did not stop
Flowing through heather, limpid brown,
Although they sat in a coffee shop
And they were neither up nor down.

The bell was silent in the air
Holding its inverted poise –
Between the clang and clang a flower,
A brazen calyx of no noise:
The bell was silent in the air.

The camels crossed the miles of sand
That stretched around the cups and plates;
The desert was their own, they planned
To portion out the stars and dates:
The camels crossed the miles of sand.

Time was away and somewhere else.
The waiter did not come, the clock
Forgot them and the radio waltz
Came out like water from a rock:
Time was away and somewhere else.

Her fingers flicked away the ash
That bloomed again in tropic trees:
Not caring if the markets crash
When they had forests such as these,
Her fingers flicked away the ash.

God or whatever means the Good
Be praised that time can stop like this,
That what the heart has understood
Can verify in the body's peace
God or whatever means the Good.

Time was away and she was here
And life no longer what it was,
The bell was silent in the air
And all the room one glow because
Time was away and she was here.

Order to View

It was a big house, bleak;
Grass on the drive;
We had been there before
But memory, weak in front of
A blistered door, could find
Nothing alive now;
The shrubbery dripped, a crypt
Of leafmould dreams; a tarnished
Arrow over an empty stable
Shifted a little in the tenuous wind,

And wishes were unable
To rise; on the garden wall
The pear trees had come loose
From rotten loops; one wish,
A rainbow bubble, rose,
Faltered, broke in the dull
Air – What was the use?
The bell-pull would not pull
And the whole place, one might
Have supposed, was deadly ill:
The world was closed,

And remained closed until
A sudden angry tree
Shook itself like a setter
Flouncing out of a pond
And beyond the sombre line
Of limes a cavalcade
Of clouds rose like a shout of
Defiance. Near at hand
Somewhere in a loose-box
A horse neighed
And all the curtains flew out of
The windows; the world was open.

from Novelettes

Les Sylphides

Life in a day: he took his girl to the ballet;
Being shortsighted himself could hardly see it –
   The white skirts in the grey
   Glade and the swell of the music
   Lifting the white sails.

Calyx upon calyx, canterbury bells in the breeze
The flowers on the left mirror to the flowers on the right
   And the naked arms above
   The powdered faces moving
   Like seaweed in a pool.

Now, he thought, we are floating – ageless, oarless –
Now there is no separation, from now on
   You will be wearing white
   Satin and a red sash
   Under the waltzing trees.

But the music stopped, the dancers took their curtain,
The river had come to a lock – a shuffle of programmes –
   And we cannot continue down
   Stream unless we are ready
   To enter the lock and drop.

So they were married – to be the more together –
And found they were never again so much together,
   Divided by the morning tea,
   By the evening paper,
   By children and tradesmen's bills.

Waking at times in the night she found assurance
Due to his regular breathing but wondered whether
   It was really worth it and where
   The river had flowed away
   And where were the white flowers.

The Gardener

He was not able to read or write,
He did odd jobs on gentlemen's places
Cutting the hedge or hoeing the drive
With the smile of a saint,
With the pride of a feudal chief,
For he was not quite all there.

Crippled by rheumatism
By the time his hair was white,
He would reach the garden by twelve
His legs in soiled puttees,
A clay pipe in his teeth,
A tiny flag in his cap,
A white cat behind him,
And his eyes a cornflower blue.

And between the clack of the shears
Or the honing of the scythe
Or the rattle of the rake on the gravel
He would talk to amuse the children,
He would talk to himself or the cat
Or the robin waiting for worms
Perched on the handle of the spade;
Would remember snatches of verse
From the elementary school
About a bee and a wasp
Or the cat by the barndoor spinning;
And would talk about himself for ever –
You would never find his like –
Always in the third person;
And would level his stick like a gun
(With a glint in his eye)
Saying 'Now I'm a Frenchman' –
He was not quite right in the head.

He believed in God –
The Good Fellow Up There –
And he used a simile of Homer

Watching the falling leaves,
And every year he waited for the Twelfth of July,
Cherishing his sash and his fife
For the carnival of banners and drums.
He was always claiming but never
Obtaining his old age pension,
For he did not know his age.

And his rheumatism at last
Kept him out of the processions.
And he came to work in the garden
Later and later in the day,
Leaving later at night;
In the damp dark of the night
At ten o'clock or later
You could hear him mowing the lawn,
The mower moving forward,
And backward, forward and backward
For he mowed while standing still;
He was not quite up to the job.

But he took a pride in the job,
He kept a bowl of cold
Tea in the crotch of a tree,
Always enjoyed his food
And enjoyed honing the scythe
And making the potato drills
And putting the peasticks in;
And enjoyed the noise of the corncrake,
And the early hawthorn hedge
Peppered black and green,
And the cut grass dancing in the air –
Happy as the day was long.

Till his last sickness took him
And he could not leave his house
And his eyes lost their colour
And he sat by the little range
With a finch in a cage and a framed
Certificate of admission
Into the Orange Order,

And his speech began to wander
And memory ebbed
Leaving upon the shore
Odd shells and heads of wrack
And his soul went out on the ebbing
Tide in a trim boat
To find the Walls of Derry
Or the land of the Ever Young.

IV

Christina

It all began so easy
With bricks upon the floor
Building motley houses
And knocking down your houses
And always building more.

The doll was called Christina,
Her underwear was lace,
She smiled while you dressed her
And when you then undressed her
She kept a smiling face.

Until the day she tumbled
And broke herself in two
And her legs and arms were hollow
And her yellow head was hollow
Behind her eyes of blue.

. . . . . .

He went to bed with a lady
Somewhere seen before,
He heard the name Christina
And suddenly saw Christina
Dead on the nursery floor.

Death of an Actress

I see from the paper that Florrie Forde is dead –
Collapsed after singing to wounded soldiers,
At the age of sixty-five. The American notice
Says no doubt all that need be said

About this one-time chorus girl; whose role
For more than forty stifling years was giving
Sexual, sentimental, or comic entertainment,
A gaudy posy for the popular soul.

Plush and cigars: she waddled into the lights,
Old and huge and painted, in velvet and tiara,
Her voice gone but around her head an aura
Of all her vanilla-sweet forgotten vaudeville nights.

With an elephantine shimmy and a sugared wink
She threw a trellis of Dorothy Perkins roses
Around an audience come from slum and suburb
And weary of the tea-leaves in the sink;

Who found her songs a rainbow leading west
To the home they never had, to the chocolate Sunday
Of boy and girl, to cowslip time, to the never-
Ending weekend Islands of the Blest.

In the Isle of Man before the war before
The present one she made a ragtime favourite
Of 'Tipperary', which became the swan-song
Of troop-ships on a darkened shore;

And during Munich sang her ancient quiz
Of *Where's Bill Bailey?* and the chorus answered,
Muddling through and glad to have no answer:
Where's Bill Bailey? How do *we* know where he is!

Now on a late and bandaged April day
In a military hospital Miss Florrie
Forde has made her positively last appearance
And taken her bow and gone correctly away.

Correctly. For she stood
For an older England, for children toddling
Hand in hand while the day was bright. Let the wren and robin
Gently with leaves cover the Babes in the Wood.

Flight of the Heart

Heart, my heart, what will you do?
There are five lame dogs and one deaf-mute
All of them with demands on you.

I will build myself a copper tower
With four ways out and no way in
But mine the glory, mine the power.

And what if the tower should shake and fall
With three sharp taps and one big bang?
What would you do with yourself at all?

I would go in the cellar and drink the dark
With two quick sips and one long pull,
Drunk as a lord and gay as a lark.

But what when the cellar roof caves in
With one blue flash and nine old bones?
How, my heart, will you save your skin?

I will go back where I belong
With one foot first and both eyes blind
I will go back where I belong
In the fore-being of mankind.

Autobiography

In my childhood trees were green
And there was plenty to be seen.

Come back early or never come.

My father made the walls resound,
He wore his collar the wrong way round.

Come back early or never come.

My mother wore a yellow dress;
Gently, gently, gentleness.

Come back early or never come.

When I was five the black dreams came;
Nothing after was quite the same.

Come back early or never come.

The dark was talking to the dead;
The lamp was dark beside my bed.

Come back early or never come.

When I woke they did not care;
Nobody, nobody was there.

Come back early or never come.

When my silent terror cried,
Nobody, nobody replied.

Come back early or never come.

I got up; the chilly sun
Saw me walk away alone.

Come back early or never come.

Conversation

Ordinary people are peculiar too:
Watch the vagrant in their eyes
Who sneaks away while they are talking with you
Into some black wood behind the skull,
Following un-, or other, realities,
Fishing for shadows in a pool.

But sometimes the vagrant comes the other way
Out of their eyes and into yours
Having mistaken you perhaps for yesterday
Or for tomorrow night, a wood in which
He may pick up among the pine-needles and burrs
The lost purse, the dropped stitch.

Vagrancy however is forbidden; ordinary men
Soon come back to normal, look you straight
In the eyes as if to say 'It will not happen again',
Put up a barrage of common sense to baulk
Intimacy but by mistake interpolate
Swear-words like roses in their talk.

The Ear

There are many sounds which are neither music nor voice,
There are many visitors in masks or in black glasses
Climbing the spiral staircase of the ear. The choice
Of callers is not ours. Behind the hedge
Of night they wait to pounce. A train passes,
The thin and audible end of a dark wedge.

We should like to lie alone in a deaf hollow
Cocoon of self where no person or thing would speak:
In fact we lie and listen as a man might follow
A will o' the wisp in an endless eyeless bog,
Follow the terrible drone of a cockchafer, or the bleak
Oracle of a barking dog.

Entered in the Minutes

I
Barcelona in Wartime

In the Paralelo a one-legged
Man sat on the ground,
His one leg out before him,
Smiling. A sudden sound

Of crazy laughter shivered
The sunlight; overhead
A parrot in a window of aspidistras
Was laughing like the dead.

II
Business Men

The two men talking business
So easily in the train
Project themselves upon me
Just as the window pane

Reflects their faces, and I
Find myself in a trance
To hear two strangers talking
The same language for once.

III
Night Club

After the legshows and the brandies
And all the pick-me-ups for tired
Men there is a feeling
Something more is required.

The lights go down and eyes
Look up across the room;
Salome comes in, bearing
The head of God knows whom.

Didymus

Refusing to fall in love with God, he gave
Himself to the love of created things,
Accepting only what he could see, a river
Full of the shadows of swallows' wings

That dipped and skimmed the water; he would not
Ask where the water ran or why.
When he died a swallow seemed to plunge
Into the reflected, the wrong, sky.

Perdita

The glamour of the end attic, the smell of old
Leather trunks – Perdita, where have you been
Hiding all these years? Somewhere or other a green
Flag is waving under an iron vault
And a brass bell is the herald of green country
And the wind is in the wires and the broom is gold.

Perdita, what became of all the things
We said that we should do? The cobwebs cover
The labels of Tyrol. The time is over-
Due and in some metropolitan station
Among the clank of cans and the roistering files
Of steam the caterpillars wait for wings.

Cradle Song for Eleanor

Sleep, my darling, sleep;
  The pity of it all
Is all we compass if
  We watch disaster fall.
Put off your twenty-odd
  Encumbered years and creep
Into the only heaven,
  The robbers' cave of sleep.

The wild grass will whisper,
  Lights of passing cars
Will streak across your dreams
  And fumble at the stars;
Life will tap the window
  Only too soon again,
Life will have her answer –
  Do not ask her when.

When the winsome bubble
  Shivers, when the bough
Breaks, will be the moment
  But not here or now.
Sleep and, asleep, forget
  The watchers on the wall
Awake all night who know
  The pity of it all.

Prayer Before Birth

I am not yet born; O hear me.
Let not the bloodsucking bat or the rat or the stoat or the
   club-footed ghoul come near me.

I am not yet born, console me.
I fear that the human race may with tall walls wall me,
   with strong drugs dope me, with wise lies lure me,
      on black racks rack me, in blood-baths roll me.

I am not yet born; provide me
With water to dandle me, grass to grow for me, trees to talk
   to me, sky to sing to me, birds and a white light
      in the back of my mind to guide me.

I am not yet born; forgive me
For the sins that in me the world shall commit, my words
   when they speak me, my thoughts when they think me,
      my treason engendered by traitors beyond me,
         my life when they murder by means of my
            hands, my death when they live me.

I am not yet born; rehearse me
In the parts I must play and the cues I must take when
   old men lecture me, bureaucrats hector me, mountains
      frown at me, lovers laugh at me, the white
         waves call me to folly and the desert calls
            me to doom and the beggar refuses
               my gift and my children curse me.

I am not yet born; O hear me,
Let not the man who is beast or who thinks he is God
   come near me.

I am not yet born; O fill me
With strength against those who would freeze my
humanity, would dragoon me into a lethal automaton,
would make me a cog in a machine, a thing with
one face, a thing, and against all those
who would dissipate my entirety, would
blow me like thistledown hither and
thither or hither and thither
like water held in the
hands would spill me.

Let them not make me a stone and let them not spill me.
Otherwise kill me.

Brother Fire

When our brother Fire was having his dog's day
Jumping the London streets with millions of tin cans
Clanking at his tail, we heard some shadow say
'Give the dog a bone' – and so we gave him ours;
Night after night we watched him slaver and crunch away
The beams of human life, the tops of topless towers.

Which gluttony of his for us was Lenten fare
Who mother-naked, suckled with sparks, were chill
Though cotted in a grille of sizzling air
Striped like a convict – black, yellow and red;
Thus were we weaned to knowledge of the Will
That wills the natural world but wills us dead.

O delicate walker, babbler, dialectician Fire,
O enemy and image of ourselves,
Did we not on those mornings after the All Clear,
When you were looting shops in elemental joy
And singing as you swarmed up city block and spire,
Echo your thought in ours? 'Destroy! Destroy!'

Neutrality

The neutral island facing the Atlantic,
The neutral island in the heart of man,
Are bitterly soft reminders of the beginnings
That ended before the end began.

Look into your heart, you will find a County Sligo,
A Knocknarea with for navel a cairn of stones,
You will find the shadow and sheen of a moleskin mountain
And a litter of chronicles and bones.

Look into your heart, you will find fermenting rivers,
Intricacies of gloom and glint,
You will find such ducats of dream and great doubloons of ceremony
As nobody today would mint.

But then look eastward from your heart, there bulks
A continent, close, dark, as archetypal sin,
While to the west off your own shores the mackerel
Are fat – on the flesh of your kin.

The Mixer

With a pert moustache and a ready candid smile
He has played his way through twenty years of pubs,
Deckchairs, lounges, touchlines, junctions, homes,
And still as ever popular, he roams
Far and narrow, mimicking the style
Of other people's leisure, scattering stubs.

Colourless, when alone, and self-accused,
He is only happy in reflected light
And only real in the range of laughter;
Behind his eyes are shadows of a night
In Flanders but his mind long since refused
To let that time intrude on what came after.

So in this second war which is fearful too,
He cannot away with silence but has grown
Almost a cipher, like a Latin word
That many languages have made their own
Till it is worn and blunt and easy to construe
And often spoken but no longer heard.

Epitaph for Liberal Poets

If in the latter
End – which is fairly soon – our way of life goes west
And some shall say *So What* and some *What Matter*,
Ready under new names to exploit or be exploited,
What, though better unsaid, would we have history say
Of us who walked in our sleep and died on our Quest?

We who always had, but never admitted, a master,
Who were expected – and paid – to be ourselves,
Conditioned to think freely, how can we
Patch up our broken hearts and modes of thought in plaster
And glorify in chromium-plated stories
Those who shall supersede us and cannot need us –
The tight-lipped technocratic Conquistadores?

The Individual has died before; Catullus
Went down young, gave place to those who were born old
And more adaptable and were not even jealous
Of his wild life and lyrics. Though our songs
Were not so warm as his, our fate is no less cold.

Such silence then before us, pinned against the wall,
Why need we whine? There is no way out, the birds
Will tell us nothing more; we shall vanish first,
Yet leave behind us certain frozen words
Which some day, though not certainly, may melt
And, for a moment or two, accentuate a thirst.

The Springboard

He never made the dive – not while I watched.
High above London, naked in the night
Perched on a board. I peered up through the bars
Made by his fear and mine but it was more than fright
That kept him crucified among the budding stars.

Yes, it was unbelief. He knew only too well
That circumstances called for sacrifice
But, shivering there, spreadeagled above the town,
His blood began to haggle over the price
History would pay if he were to throw himself down.

If it would mend the world, that would be worth while
But he, quite rightly, long had ceased to believe
In any Utopia or in Peace-upon-Earth;
His friends would find in his death neither ransom nor reprieve
But only a grain of faith – for what it was worth.

And yet we know he knows what he must do.
There above London where the gargoyles grin
He will dive like a bomber past the broken steeple,
One man wiping out his own original sin
And, like ten million others, dying for the people.

The Casualty

(in memoriam G. H. S.)

'Damn!' you would say if I were to write the best
Tribute I could to you, 'All clichés', and you would grin
Dwindling to where that faded star allures
Where no time presses and no days begin –
Turning back shrugging to the misty West
Remembered out of Homer but now yours.

Than whom I do not expect ever again
To find a more accordant friend, with whom
I could be silent knowledgeably; you never
Faked or flattered or time-served. If ten
Winds were to shout you down or twenty oceans boom
Above the last of you, they will not sever

That thread of so articulate silence. How
You died remains conjecture; instantaneous
Is the most likely – that the shutter fell
Congealing the kaleidoscope at Now
And making all your past contemporaneous
Under that final chord of the mid-Atlantic swell.

So now the concert is over, the seats vacated,
Eels among the footlights, water up to the roof
And the gilded cherubs crumbling – and you come in
Jaunty as ever but with a half-frustrated
Look on your face, you expect the show to begin
But you are too late and cannot accept the proof

That you are too late because you have died too early
And this is under sea. Puzzled but gay
You still come in, come in, and the waves distort
Your smile and chivvy your limbs through a maze of pearly
Pillars of ocean death – and yet you force your way
In on my dreams as if you had something still to report.

How was it then? How is it? You and I
Have often since we were children discussed death
And sniggered at the preacher and wondered how
He can talk so big about mortality
And immortality more. But you yourself could now
Talk big as any – if you had the breath.

However since you cannot from this date
Talk big or little, since you cannot answer
Even what alive you could, but I let slip
The chance to ask you, I can correlate
Only of you what memories dart and trip
Through freckling lights and stop like a forgetful dancer.

Archaic gusto sprouted from a vase
Of dancing satyrs, lips of a Gothic imp
Laughing down from a church-top, inky fingers
Jotting notes on notes, and piccolo and tymp
Importunate at the circus – but there lingers
Also a scent of awe, a cosmic pause;

For you were a good mixer and could laugh
With Rowlandson or Goya and you liked
Bijoux and long-eared dogs and silken legs
And titivated rooms but more than half
Your story lay outside beyond the spiked
Railing where in the night some old blind minstrel begs.

He begged and you responded, being yourself,
Like Raftery or Homer, of his kind –
Creative not for the counter or the shelf
But innocently whom the world bewilders
And so they observe and love it till their mind
May turn them from mere students into builders.

Of which high humble company were you,
Outside the cliques, unbothered with the fashion,
And self-apprenticed to the grinding trade
Of thinking things anew, stropping the blade
You never used, your multicoloured passion
Having been merged by death in universal Blue.

So what you gave were inklings: trivial signs
Of some momentous truth, a footprint here and there
In melting snow, a marginal caress
Of someone else's words, a gentleness
In greeting, a panache of heady wines
Or children's rockets vanishing in air.

Look at these snapshots; here you see yourself
Spilling a paint-pot on a virgin wall
Or boisterous in a sailing-boat or bubbling
At a Punch-and-Judy show or a music-hall
Or lugging Clausewitz from a public shelf
To make your private notes, thumbing and doubling

His corseted pages back. Yes, here and here
You see yourself spilling across the border
Of nice convention, here at a students' dance
Pinching a girl's behind – to reappear
A small boy twined in bracken and aprance
Like any goatfoot faun to propagate disorder.

Here you are swapping gags in winking bars
With half an eye on the colour clash of beet
Lobster and radish, here you are talking back
To a caged baboon and here the Wiltshire sleet
Riddles your football jersey – here the sack
Of night pours down on you Provençal stars.

Here you are gabbling Baudelaire or Donne,
Here you are mimicking that cuckoo clock,
Here you are serving a double fault for set,
Here you are diving naked from a Dalmatian rock,
Here you are barracking the sinking sun,
Here you are taking Proust aboard your doomed corvette.

Yes, all you gave were inklings; even so
Invaluable – such as I remember
Out of your mouth or only in your eyes
On walks in blowsy August, Brueghel-like December,
Or when the gas was hissing and a glow
Of copper jugs gave back your lyrical surprise.

For above all that was your gift – to be
Surprised and therefore sympathetic, warm
Towards things as well as people, you could see
The integrity of differences – O did you
Make one last integration, find a Form
Grow out of formlessness when the Atlantic hid you?

Whether you did or not, the fact remains
(Which I, for all your doubts, could have no doubt of)
That your whole life till then showed an endeavour
Towards a discovery – and if your pains
Were lost the loss is ours as well; for you are out of
This life and cannot start any more hares for ever.

When We Were Children

When we were children words were coloured
(Harlot and murder were dark purple)
And language was a prism, the light
   A conjured inlay on the grass,
Whose rays today are concentrated
   And language grown a burning-glass.

When we were children Spring was easy,
Dousing our heads in suds of hawthorn
And scrambling the laburnum tree –
   A breakfast for the gluttonous eye;
Whose winds and sweets have now forsaken
   Lungs that are black, tongues that are dry.

Now we are older and our talents
Accredited to time and meaning,
To handsel joy requires a new
   Shuffle of cards behind the brain
Where meaning shall remarry colour
   And flowers be timeless once again.

Corner Seat

Suspended in a moving night
The face in the reflected train
Looks at first sight as self-assured
As your own face – But look again:

Windows between you and the world
Keep out the cold, keep out the fright;
Then why does your reflection seem
So lonely in the moving night?

Carrick Revisited

Back to Carrick, the castle as plumb assured
As thirty years ago – Which war was which?
Here are new villas, here is a sizzling grid
But the green banks are as rich and the lough as hazily lazy
And the child's astonishment not yet cured.

Who was – and am – dumbfounded to find myself
In a topographical frame – here, not there –
The channels of my dreams determined largely
By random chemistry of soil and air;
Memories I had shelved peer at me from the shelf.

Fog-horn, mill-horn, corncrake and church bell
Half-heard through boarded time as a child in bed
Glimpses a brangle of talk from the floor below
But cannot catch the words. Our past we know
But not its meaning – whether it meant well.

Time and place – our bridgeheads into reality
But also its concealment! Out of the sea
We land on the Particular and lose
All other possible bird's-eye views, the Truth
That is of Itself for Itself – but not for me.

Torn before birth from where my fathers dwelt,
Schooled from the age of ten to a foreign voice,
Yet neither western Ireland nor southern England
Cancels this interlude; what chance misspelt
May never now be righted by my choice.

Whatever then my inherited or acquired
Affinities, such remains my childhood's frame
Like a belated rock in the red Antrim clay
That cannot at this era change its pitch or name –
And the pre-natal mountain is far away.

The Strand

White Tintoretto clouds beneath my naked feet,
This mirror of wet sand imputes a lasting mood
To island truancies; my steps repeat

Someone's who now has left such strands for good
Carrying his boots and paddling like a child,
A square black figure whom the horizon understood –

My father. Who for all his responsibly compiled
Account books of a devout, precise routine
Kept something in him solitary and wild,

So loved the western sea and no tree's green
Fulfilled him like these contours of Slievemore
Menaun and Croaghaun and the bogs between.

Sixty-odd years behind him and twelve before,
Eyeing the flange of steel in the turning belt of brine
It was sixteen years ago he walked this shore

And the mirror caught his shape which catches mine
But then as now the floor-mop of the foam
Blotted the bright reflections – and no sign

Remains of face or feet when visitors have gone home.

Last before America

A spiral of green hay on the end of a rake:
The moment is sweat and sun-prick – children and old women
Big in a tiny field, midgets against the mountain,
So toy-like yet so purposed you could take
This for the Middle Ages.

At night the accordion melts in the wind from the sea
From the bourne of emigrant uncle and son, a defeated
Music that yearns and abdicates; chimney-smoke and spindrift
Mingle and part as ghosts do. The decree
Of the sea's divorce is final.

Pennsylvania or Boston? It was another name,
A land of a better because an impossible promise
Which split these families; it was to be a journey
Away from death – yet the travellers died the same
As those who stayed in Ireland.

Both myth and seismic history have been long suppressed
Which made and unmade Hy Brasil – now an image
For those who despise charts but find their dream's endorsement
In certain long low islets snouting towards the west
Like cubs that have lost their mother.

Western Landscape

In doggerel and stout let me honour this country
Though the air is so soft that it smudges the words
And herds of great clouds find the gaps in the fences
Of chance preconceptions and foam-quoits on rock-points
At once hit and miss, hit and miss.
So the kiss of the past is narcotic, the ocean
Lollingly lullingly over-insidiously
Over and under crossing the eyes
And docking the queues of the teetotum consciousness
Proves and disproves what it wants.
For the western climate is Lethe,
The smoky taste of cooking on turf is lotus,
There are affirmation and abnegation together
From the broken bog with its veins of amber water,
From the distant headland, a sphinx's fist, that barely grips the sea,
From the taut-necked donkey's neurotic-asthmatic-erotic lamenting,
From the heron in trance and in half-mourning,
From the mitred mountain weeping shale.

O grail of emerald passing light
And hanging smell of sweetest hay
And grain of sea and loom of wind
Weavingly laughingly leavingly weepingly –
Webs that will last and will not.
But what
Is the hold upon, the affinity with
Ourselves of such a light and line,
How do we find continuance
Of our too human skeins of wish
In this inhuman effluence?
O relevance of cloud and rock –
If such could be our permanence!
The flock of mountain sheep belong
To tumbled screes, to tumbling seas
The ribboned wrack, and moor to mist;
But we who savour longingly
This plentitude of solitude
Have lost the right to residence,
Can only glean ephemeral

Ears of our once beatitude.
Caressingly cajolingly –
Take what you can for soon you go –
Consolingly, coquettishly,
The soft rain kisses and forgets,
Silken mesh on skin and mind;
A deaf-dumb siren that can sing
With fingertips her falsities,
Welcoming, abandoning.

O Brandan, spindrift hermit, who
Hankering roaming un-homing up-anchoring
From this rock wall looked seawards to
Knot the horizon round your waist,
Distil that distance and undo
Time in quintessential West:
The best negation, round as nought,
Stiller than stolen sleep – though bought
With mortification, voiceless choir
Where all were silent as one man
And all desire fulfilled, unsought.
Thought:
The curragh went over the wave and dipped in the trough
When that horny-handed saint with the abstract eye set off
Which was fourteen hundred years ago – maybe never –
And yet he bobs beyond that next high crest for ever.
Feeling:
Sea met sky, he had neither floor nor ceiling,
The rising blue of turf-smoke and mountain were left behind,
Blue neither upped nor downed, there was blue all round the mind.
Emotion:
One thought of God, one feeling of the ocean,
Fused in the moving body, the unmmoved soul,
Made him a part of a not to be parted whole.
Whole.
And the West was all the world, the lonely was the only,
The chosen – and there was no choice – the Best,
For the beyond was here . . .

But for us now
The beyond is still out there as on tiptoes here we stand
On promontories that are themselves a-tiptoe

Reluctant to be land. Which is why this land
Is always more than matter – as a ballet
Dancer is more than body. The west of Ireland
Is brute and ghost at once. Therefore in passing
Among these shadows of this permanent show
Flitting evolving dissolving but never quitting –
This arbitrary and necessary Nature
Both bountiful and callous, harsh and wheedling –
Let now the visitor, although disfranchised
In the constituencies of quartz and bog-oak
And ousted from the elemental congress,
Let me at least in token that my mother
Earth was a rocky earth with breasts uncovered
To suckle solitary intellects
And limber instincts, let me, if a bastard
Out of the West by urban civilization
(Which unwished father claims me – so I must take
What I can before I go) let me who am neither Brandan
Free of all roots nor yet a rooted peasant
Here add one stone to the indifferent cairn . . .
With a stone on the cairn, with a word on the wind, with a prayer in
the flesh let me honour this country.

Under the Mountain

Seen from above
The foam in the curving bay is a goose-quill
That feathers . . . unfeathers . . . itself.

Seen from above
The field is a flap and the haycocks buttons
To keep it flush with the earth.

Seen from above
The house is a silent gadget whose purpose
Was long since obsolete.

But when you get down
The breakers are cold scum and the wrack
Sizzles with stinking life.

When you get down
The field is a failed or a worth-while crop, the source
Of back-ache if not heartache.

And when you get down
The house is a maelstrom of loves and hates where you –
Having got down – belong.

The Cyclist

Freewheeling down the escarpment past the unpassing horse
Blazoned in chalk the wind he causes in passing
Cools the sweat of his neck, making him one with the sky,
In the heat of the handlebars he grasps the summer
Being a boy and today a parenthesis
Between the horizon's brackets; the main sentence
Waits to be picked up later but these five minutes
Are all today and summer. The dragonfly
Rises without take-off, horizontal,
Underlining itself in a sliver of peacock light.

And glaring, glaring white
The horse on the down moves within his brackets,
The grass boils with grasshoppers, a pebble
Scutters from under the wheel and all this country
Is spattered white with boys riding their heat-wave,
Feet on a narrow plank and hair thrown back

And a surf of dust beneath them. Summer, summer –
They chase it with butterfly nets or strike it into the deep
In a little red ball or gulp it lathered with cream
Or drink it through closed eyelids; until the bell
Left-right-left gives his forgotten sentence
And reaching the valley the boy must pedal again
Left-right-left but meanwhile
For ten seconds more can move as the horse in the chalk
Moves unbeginningly calmly
Calmly regardless of tenses and final clauses
Calmly unendingly moves.

Woods

My father who found the English landscape tame
Had hardly in his life walked in a wood,
Too old when first he met one; Malory's knights,
Keats's nymphs or the Midsummer Night's Dream
Could never arras the room, where he spelled out True and Good
With their interleaving of half-truths and not-quites.

While for me from the age of ten the socketed wooden gate
Into a Dorset planting, into a dark
But gentle ambush, was an alluring eye;
Within was a kingdom free from time and sky,
Caterpillar webs on the forehead, danger under the feet,
And the mind adrift in a floating and rustling ark

Packed with birds and ghosts, two of every race,
Trills of love from the picture-book – Oh might I never land
But here, grown six foot tall, find me also a love
Also out of the picture-book; whose hand
Would be soft as the webs of the wood and on her face
The wood-pigeon's voice would shaft a chrism from above.

So in a grassy ride a rain-filled hoof-mark coined
By a finger of sun from the mint of Long Ago
Was the last of Lancelot's glitter. Make-believe dies hard;
That the rider passed here lately and is a man we know
Is still untrue, the gate to Legend remains unbarred,
The grown-up hates to divorce what the child joined.

Thus from a city when my father would frame
Escape, he thought, as I do, of bog or rock
But I have also this other, this English, choice
Into what yet is foreign; whatever its name
Each wood is the mystery and the recurring shock
Of its dark coolness is a foreign voice.

Yet in using the word tame my father was maybe right,
These woods are not the Forest; each is moored
To a village somewhere near. If not of today
They are not like the wilds of Mayo, they are assured
Of their place by men; reprieved from the neolithic night
By gamekeepers or by Herrick's girls at play.

And always we walk out again. The patch
Of sky at the end of the path grows and discloses
An ordered open air long ruled by dyke and fence,
With geese whose form and gait proclaim their consequence,
Pargetted outposts, windows browed with thatch,
And cow pats – and inconsequent wild roses.

Elegy for Minor Poets

Who often found their way to pleasant meadows
Or maybe once to a peak, who saw the Promised Land,
Who took the correct three strides but tripped their hurdles,
Who had some prompter they barely could understand,
Who were too happy or sad, too soon or late,
I would praise these in company with the Great;

For if not in the same way, they fingered the same language
According to their lights. For them as for us
Chance was a coryphaeus who could be either
An angel or an *ignis fatuus*.
Let us keep our mind open, our fingers crossed;
Some who go dancing through dark bogs are lost.

Who were lost in many ways, through comfort, lack of knowledge,
Or between women's breasts, who thought too little, too much,
Who were the world's best talkers, in tone and rhythm
Superb, yet as writers lacked a sense of touch,
So either gave up or just went on and on –
Let us salute them now their chance is gone;

And give the benefit of the doubtful summer
To those who worshipped the sky but stayed indoors
Bound to a desk by conscience or by the spirit's
Hayfever. From those office and study floors
Let the sun clamber on to the notebook, shine,
And fill in what they groped for between each line.

Who were too carefree or careful, who were too many
Though always few and alone, who went the pace
But ran in circles, who were lamed by fashion,
Who lived in the wrong time or the wrong place,
Who might have caught fire had only a spark occurred,
Who knew all the words but failed to achieve the Word –

Their ghosts are gagged, their books are library flotsam,
Some of their names – not all – we learnt in school
But, life being short, we rarely read their poems,
Mere source-books now to point or except a rule,
While those opinions which rank them high are based
On a wish to be different or on lack of taste.

In spite of and because of which, we later
Suitors to their mistress (who, unlike them, stays young)
Do right to hang on the grave of each a trophy
Such as, if solvent, he would himself have hung
Above himself; these debtors preclude our scorn –
Did we not underwrite them when we were born?

Autolycus

In his last phase when hardly bothering
To be a dramatist, the Master turned away
From his taut plots and complex characters
To tapestried romances, conjuring
With rainbow names and handfuls of sea-spray
And from them turned out happy Ever-afters.

Eclectic always, now extravagant,
Sighting his matter through a timeless prism
He ranged his classical bric-à-brac in grottoes
Where knights of Ancient Greece had Latin mottoes
And fishermen their flapjacks – none should want
Colour for lack of an anachronism.

A gay world certainly though pocked and scored
With childish horrors and a fresh world though
Its mainsprings were old gags – babies exposed,
Identities confused and queens to be restored;
But when the cracker bursts it proves as you supposed –
Trinket and moral tumble out just so.

Such innocence – In his own words it was
Like an old tale, only that where time leaps
Between acts three and four there was something born
Which made the stock-type virgin dance like corn
In a wind that having known foul marshes, barren steeps,
Felt therefore kindly towards Marinas, Perditas . . .

Thus crystal learned to talk. But Shakespeare balanced it
With what we knew already, gabbing earth
Hot from Eastcheap – Watch your pockets when
That rogue comes round the corner, he can slit
Purse-strings as quickly as his maker's pen
Will try your heartstrings in the name of mirth.

O master pedlar with your confidence tricks,
Brooches, pomanders, broadsheets and what-have-you,
Who hawk such entertainment but rook your client
And leave him brooding, why should we forgive you
Did we not know that, though more self-reliant
Than we, you too were born and grew up in a fix?

Slow Movement

Waking, he found himself in a train, andante,
With wafers of early sunlight blessing the unknown fields
And yesterday cancelled out, except for yesterday's papers
    Huddling under the seat.

It is still very early, this is a slow movement;
The viola-player's hand like a fish in a glass tank
Rises, remains quivering, darts away
    To nibble invisible weeds.

Great white nebulae lurch against the window
To deploy across the valley, the children are not yet up
To wave us on – we pass without spectators,
    Braiding a voiceless creed.

And the girl opposite, name unknown, is still
Asleep and the colour of her eyes unknown
Which might be wells of sun or moons of wish
    But it is still very early.

The movement ends, the train has come to a stop
In buttercup fields, the fiddles are silent, the whole
Shoal of silver tessellates the aquarium
    Floor, not a bubble rises . . .

And what happens next on the programme we do not know,
If, the red line topped on the gauge, the fish will go mad in the tank
Accelerando con forza, the sleeper open her eyes
    And, so doing, open ours.

from Day of Returning

But even so, he said, daily I hanker, daily
Ache to get back to my home, to see my day of returning
After those years of violent action – and these of inaction.
Always and even so. But I have no ship, no comrades,
Only my wits with nothing to grind on. Nectar, ambrosia,
Promise me nothing; the goddess no longer pleases me.
Who would be loved by a goddess for long? Hours which are golden
But unreal hours, flowers which forget to fall,
And wine too smooth, no wrinkles to match my own –
Who would be loved by a goddess who cannot appreciate
The joy of solving a problem, who never wept
For friends that she used to laugh with? I stare at the sea
Till that hard horizon rounds one great round eye
Hard as that of the Cyclops; this time I have no
Means of putting it out – and now I am really No Man
For my ears ring with a too sweet voice which never
Falters or ages. They call me crafty Odysseus;
I have used my craft on gods and nymphs and demigods
But it is time, high time, I turned it again
To the earth that bred it, a new threshing floor
Or setting up boundary stones, for even the best
Neighbours encroach – and I like to have someone to argue with
About my rights of grazing or wood-cutting; aye, it is time
I heard the bleat of my goats and smelt the dung of my cattle;
Here there is neither dung nor rights nor argument,
Only the scent of flowers and a too sweet voice which is ever
Youthful and fails to move me. Here could never be home,
No more than the sea around it. And even the sea
Is a different sea round Ithaca.

from Flowers in the Interval

III

Because you intoxicate like all the drinks
We have drunk together from Achill Island to Athens,
Retsina or Nostrano, pops and clinks

Through snow or mist or mistral, aquavit
Or Château Neuf du Pape, from coloured inks
To the blood of bulls or sun-gods, dry or sweet,

Bitter or mild, armagnac, ouzo, stout,
Because, like each of these, you reprieve, repeat
Whether dry or sweet your newness, with or without

Water, and each one ray of you distils
A benediction and an end to doubt
Because your presence is all rays and rills;

Because your presence is baths of freesias, because
Your eyes are the gold-flecked loughs of Irish hills,
Your hands are Parvati and Millamant and what was

The earliest corn-and-fire dance is your hair,
Your stance is a caryatid's who seems to pause
Before she slips off, blandly unaware

Of the architrave on her head, because your moods
Are sun and water and because the air
Is burnished by you and the multitudes

Of humble moments answer to your voice
Like goldfish to a bell or sleeping woods
To a fresh breeze, because you make no choice

Unless you feel it first, because your laugh
Is Catherine wheels and dolphins, because Rejoice
Is etched upon your eyes, because the chaff

Of dead wit flies before you and the froth
Of false convention with it, because you are half
Night and half day, both woven in one cloth,

Because your colours are onyx and cantaloupe,
Wet seaweed, lizard, lilac, tiger-moth
And olive groves and beech-woods, because you scoop

The sun up in your hands, because your form
Is bevelled hills which neither crane nor stoop,
Because your voice is carved of jade yet warm

And always is itself and always new,
A pocket of calm air amidst a storm
And yet a ripple beneath all calms, a view

Into wide space which still is near; is you.

from Autumn Sequel

from Canto XVII

This was the night that specially we went down,
When we were small, to the kitchen where the cook,
A Catholic farmer's daughter from Fivemiletown,

Poked up the fire in the open range and took
Her apron off and dropped her crochet work
And dropped the apples in the tub and shook

The lamplight with her laughter; quiz and quirk,
Riddle and slapstick, kept the dark at bay
Though ghosts and goblins, we well knew, must lurk

No further off than the scullery and today
The bogs, the black domain of the Will o' the Wisp,
Had closed in round our house from miles away.

No matter; apples were sharp and nuts were crisp,
She practised divination with cups of tea
And we responded in a childish lisp

To what our future brides or grooms should be,
And cracking nut on nut were unaware
Of the god that grinned at us from the hazel tree.

An ancient Celtic world had filled the air,
The cropped black sow was lurking at the gate
To seize the hindmost, and the empty chair

That creaked was creaking from the unseen weight
Of some dead man who thought this New Year's Eve,
The Celtic world having known a different date.

The white ash dropped; the night kept up its sleeve
The Queen of Apples, the Ace of Fires, the Jack
Of Coffins, and one joker. Soon we should have to leave

The lamplight and the firelight and climb back
Into our small cold beds with a small cold
Wind that made the blind in the window clack

And soot fall down the chimney on to the six-months-old
Newspaper frill in the fireplace. Climbing asleep in the snow
Of the sheets I remembered again what I had been often told:

'Aye, you are here now – but you never know
Where you will be when you wake up.' I lay
Fearing the night through till the cock should crow

To tell me that my fears were swept away
And tomorrow had come again. So now I wake
To find that it is Norwich and All Saints' Day,

All devils and fancy spent, only an ache
Where once there was an anguish. The tall spire
In harsh grey rain stands grey while great gales shake

The trees of Tombland; every man's desire
Is washed away in what is a record fall
Of rain, as the gay colours of nave and choir

Were washed away long since. The church bells call
Forlornly from their cages within cages,
Oak beams within blind stone; a similar wall

Immures for each of us the Middle Ages
Of our own childhood; centuries of rain
Have made the colours run and swilled the pages

Whether of missal or chapbook down the drain
In one conglomerate pulp; the distant chimes
Have ceased to hold us in their tangled skein

Since we must have our worlds as in our times
And, if we once looked back, might turn to stone
Like all the saints. The reasons and the rhymes

Of Mother Church and Mother Goose have grown
Equally useless since we have grown up
And learnt to call our minds (if minds they are) our own,

And neither need a special spoon to sup
With the devil any more nor need to forage,
As lepers did, for scraps with clapper and cup;

We know no leper, or devil, remains in Norwich
And that, however rashly one proceeds,
One cannot burn one's mouth with cold plum porridge.

from Canto xx

To Wales once more, though not on holiday now;
Glued to my seat, whirled down a ruthless track
To Wales once more, grasping a golden bough,

Key to the misty west. I am wearing black
Shoes which I bought with Gwilym in Regent Street
To travel to Drumcliff in, five years back;

Drumcliff was wet, those new shoes cramped my feet
At Yeats's funeral; they are not so smart
Nor yet so tight for Gwilym's.

*   *   *

The river rolls on west
As proud and clear as its best years have rolled

And lands us at the village, which is dressed
In one uncanny quiet and one kind
Blue sky, an attitude of host to guest

Saying: Come share my grief. We walk behind
The slow great heaps of flowers, the small austere
And single laurel wreath. But the numbed mind

Fails to accept such words as tempt the ear –
The Resurrection and the Life; it knows
Only that Gwilym once was living here

And here is now being buried. A repose
Of sunlight lies on the green sloping field
Which should hold goats or geese. My fingers close

On what green thoughts this acre still can yield
Before we leave that deep, that not green, grave,
That letter to be superscribed and sealed

Now that it has no contents; wind and wave
Retain far more of Gwilym. What he took
From this small corner of Wales survives in what he gave.

The green field empties, with one tentative look
Backwards we move away, and then walk down
To where he lived on a cliff; an open book

Of sands and waters, silver and shining brown,
His estuary spreads before us and its birds
To which he gave renown reflect renown

On him, their cries resolve into his words
Just as, upon the right, Sir John's just hill
Looks now, and justly, Gwilym's. We leave the curds

And crimps of flats and channels and through the still
Evening rejoin the mourners. If a birth
Extends a family circle and glasses fill

Confirming its uniqueness and the worth
Of life, I think a death too does the same,
Confirming and extending. Earth to earth,

But to the whole of it. In Gwilym's name
We talk and even laugh, though now and then
Illusions (surely illusions?) rise, to shame

My reason. Three illusions. One: that when
We left that grassy field, we also left
Gwilym behind there, if not able to pen

One word, yet able perhaps to feel bereft
Or maybe to feel pleased that such a place
Remains to him. Then was it gift or theft,

This burial? More rational thoughts efface
Such whims, but the second illusion comes: perhaps
Gwilym has slipped off somewhere, into the grace

Of some afterlife where free from toils and traps
He revels for ever in words. These fancies too
Flicker like Will o' the Wistfuls, and collapse;

Since, even if an afterlife were true,
Gwilym without his body, his booming voice,
Would simply not be Gwilym. As I or you

Would not be I or you and, given the choice,
I, for one, would reject it. Last, the third
Illusion, which gives reason to rejoice

Or rather strong unreason: what we have heard
And seen today means nothing, this crowded bar
Was one of Gwilym's favourites, it is absurd

He should not join us here, it was always going too far
To expect him on the dot but, late or soon,
He will come jaunting in, especially as there are

So many of his friends here to buffoon
And sparkle with. However, if not tonight,
We need not wait for leap year or blue moon

Before we run across him. Moons are white
In London as in Wales and by tomorrow
We shall be back in London where the sight

And sound of him will be welcome, he may borrow
A pound or two of course or keep us waiting
But what about it? In those streets of sorrow

[124]

And even more of boredom, his elating
Elated presence brings a sluice of fresh
Water into dim ponds too long stagnating.

This is the third illusion, a fine mesh
Of probable impossibles; of course,
Of course, we think, we shall meet him in the flesh

Tomorrow or the next day, in full force
Of flesh and wit and heart. We close the door
On Wales and backwards, eastwards, from the source

Of such clear water, leave that altered shore
Of gulls and psalms, of green and gold largesse.
November the Twenty-fifth. We are back once more

In London. And will he keep us waiting? . . . Yes.

To Posterity

When books have all seized up like the books in graveyards
And reading and even speaking have been replaced
By other, less difficult, media, we wonder if you
Will find in flowers and fruit the same colour and taste
They held for us for whom they were framed in words,
And will your grass be green, your sky be blue,
Or will your birds be always wingless birds?

from A Hand of Snapshots

The Left-Behind

Peering into your stout you see a past of lazybeds,
A liner moving west, leaving the husk of home,
Its white wake lashing round your pimpled haycocks.
Drink up, Rip MacWinkle. The night is old.

Where can you find a fire that burns and gives no warmth?
Where is the tall ship that chose to run on a rock?
Where are there more fish than ever filled the ocean?
Where can you find a clock that strikes when it has stopped?

Oh, poverty is the fire that burns and gives no warmth.
My youth is the tall ship that chose to run on a rock.
Men yet unborn could more than fill the ocean,
And death is the black clock that strikes when it has stopped.

My glass is low and I lack money to fill it,
I gaze on the black dregs and the yellow scum,
And the night is old and a nightbird calls me away
To what now is merely mine, and soon will be no one's home.

The Back-Again

Back for his holiday from across the water
He fishes with spinners or a rubber eel,
Fishes for mackerel or pollock, but also for something
That he remembers now more by the feel
Of the jigging line than by how it looked when landed.

If it was ever landed. Sitting beside his father,
Whose eyes are smoored with distance, he talks of crops
And weather but would prefer to talk of something
For which he has no words. Till the talk stops
And the fire inside and the rain outside are silent.

And his thoughts return to the city as he fingers
His city tie, thinking he has made good,
Gone up in the world, on the whole, were it not for something,
Intuited perhaps though never understood,
Which flitted through this room around his cradle.

So, on his last day, walking beside his brother,
Whose dog like a black thought streaks through ditch and fence
Rounding up sheep, he sees in his brother a sudden something:
An oaf, but an oaf with dignity and the sense
That it is a fine day if it rains only a little.

The Once-in-Passing

And here the cross on the window means myself
But that window does not open;
Born here, I should have proved a different self.
Such vistas dare not open;
For what can walk or talk without tongue or feet?

Here for a month to spend but not to earn,
How could I even imagine
Such a life here that my plain days could earn
The life my dreams imagine?
For what takes root or grows that owns no root?

Yet here for a month, and for this once in passing,
I can imagine at least
The permanence of what passes,
As though the window opened
And the ancient cross on the hillside meant myself.

Beni Hasan

It came to me on the Nile my passport lied
Calling me dark who am grey. In the brown cliff
A row of tombs, of portholes, stared and stared as if
They were the long-dead eyes of beasts inside
Time's cage, black eyes on eyes that stared away
Lion-like focused on some different day
On which, on a long-term view, it was I, not they, had died.

The Tree of Guilt

When first we knew it, gibbet-bare
It scrawled an omen on the air,
But later, in its wealth of leaf,
Looked too lush to hang a thief;

And from its branches muffled doves
Drummed out the purchasable loves
Which far below them were purveyed
On credit through the slinking shade.

And what a cooing trade was done
Around the tree-trunk anyone
Could guess who saw the countless hearts
Carved in its bark transfixed with darts;

So entering this enchanted zone
Anyone would add his own
Cut neatly with a pocket knife,
There for his life and the tree's life.

And having thus signed on the line
Anyone claimed his anodyne
And, drinking it, was lulled asleep
By doves and insects, deep and deep,

Till he finds later, waking cold,
The leaves fallen, himself old,
And his carved heart, though vastly grown,
Not recognizably his own.

The dove's is now the raven's day
And there is interest yet to pay;
And in those branches, gibbet-bare,
Is that a noose that dangles there?

House on a Cliff

Indoors the tang of a tiny oil lamp. Outdoors
The winking signal on the waste of sea.
Indoors the sound of the wind. Outdoors the wind.
Indoors the locked heart and the lost key.

Outdoors the chill, the void, the siren. Indoors
The strong man pained to find his red blood cools,
While the blind clock grows louder, faster. Outdoors
The silent moon, the garrulous tides she rules.

Indoors ancestral curse-cum-blessing. Outdoors
The empty bowl of heaven, the empty deep.
Indoors a purposeful man who talks at cross
Purposes, to himself, in a broken sleep.

Figure of Eight

In the top and front of a bus, eager to meet his fate,
He pressed with foot and mind to gather speed,
Then, when the lights were changing, jumped and hurried,
Though dead on time, to the meeting place agreed,
But there was no one there. He chose to wait.
No one came. He need not perhaps have worried.

Whereas today in the rear and gloom of a train,
Loath, loath to meet his fate, he cowers and prays
For some last-minute hitch, some unheard-of abdication,
But, winding up the black thread of his days,
The wheels roll on and make it all too plain
Who will be there to meet him at the station.

Death of an Old Lady

At five in the morning there were grey voices
Calling three times through the dank fields;
The ground fell away beyond the voices
Forty long years to the wrinkled lough
That had given a child one shining glimpse
Of a boat so big it was named Titanic.

Named or called? For a name is a call –
Shipyard voices at five in the morning,
As now for this old tired lady who sails
Towards her own iceberg calm and slow;
We hardly hear the screws, we hardly
Can think her back her four score years.

They called and ceased. Later the night nurse
Handed over, the day went down
To the sea in a ship, it was grey April,
The daffodils in her garden waited
To make her a wreath, the iceberg waited;
At eight in the evening the ship went down.

Apple Blossom

The first blossom was the best blossom
For the child who never had seen an orchard;
For the youth whom whisky had led astray
The morning after was the first day.

The first apple was the best apple
For Adam before he heard the sentence;
When the flaming sword endorsed the Fall
The trees were his to plant for all.

The first ocean was the best ocean
For the child from streets of doubt and litter;
For the youth for whom the skies unfurled
His first love was his first world.

But the first verdict seemed the worst verdict
When Adam and Eve were expelled from Eden;
Yet when the bitter gates clanged to
The sky beyond was just as blue.

For the next ocean is the first ocean
And the last ocean is the first ocean
And, however often the sun may rise,
A new thing dawns upon our eyes.

For the last blossom is the first blossom
And the first blossom is the best blossom
And when from Eden we take our way
The morning after is the first day.

The Riddle

'What is it that goes round and round the house'
The riddle began. A wolf, we thought, or a ghost?
Our cold backs turned to the chink in the kitchen shutter,
The range made our small scared faces warm as toast.

But now the cook is dead and the cooking, no doubt, electric,
No room for draught or dream, for child or mouse,
Though we, in another place, still put ourselves the question:
What *is* it that goes round and round the house?

The Slow Starter

A watched clock never moves, they said:
Leave it alone and you'll grow up.
Nor will the sulking holiday train
Start sooner if you stamp your feet.
    He left the clock to go its way;
    The whistle blew, the train went gay.

Do not press me so, she said;
Leave me alone and I will write
But not just yet, I am sure you know
The problem. Do not count the days.
    He left the calendar alone;
    The postman knocked, no letter came.

O never force the pace, they said;
Leave it alone, you have lots of time,
Your kind of work is none the worse
For slow maturing. Do not rush.
    He took their tip, he took his time,
    And found his time and talent gone.

Oh you have had your chance, It said;
Left it alone and it was one.
Who said a watched clock never moves?
Look at it now. Your chance was I.
    He turned and saw the accusing clock
    Race like a torrent round a rock.

from Dark Age Glosses

on the Venerable Bede

Birds flitting in and out of the barn
Bring back an Anglo-Saxon story:
The great wooden hall with long fires down the centre,
Their feet in the rushes, their hands tearing the meat.
Suddenly high above them they notice a swallow enter
From the black storm and zigzag over their heads,
Then out once more into the unknown night;
And that, someone remarks, is the life of man.
But now it is time to sleep; one by one
They rise from the bench and their gigantic shadows
Lurch on the shuddering walls. How can the world
Or the non-world beyond harbour a bird?
They close their eyes that smart from the woodsmoke: how
Can anyone even guess his whence and whither?
This indoors flying makes it seem absurd,
Although it itches and nags and flutters and yearns,
To postulate any other life than now.

on the Four Masters

The light was no doubt the same, the ecology different:
All Ireland drowned in woods. Those who today
Think it a golden age and at Glendalough
Or Clonmacnois let imagination play
Like flame upon those ruins should keep in mind
That the original actual flames were often
Kindled not by the Norsemen but by the monks'
Compatriots, boorish kings who, mad to find
Loot to outride each other's ambition, would stop
At nothing – which so often led to nothing.
Which is even – tell it not in the Gaelic League –
True of the High King Brian whose eighty years,
Caught in a web of largely his own intrigue,
Soured him with power and rusted him with blood
To let him die in a tent on a cold Good Friday
To earn his niche. And yet he earned his niche.

The last battle was his; maybe the sun came out
Before the defeated Norseman struck him, before
History endorsed the triumph and the rout.
The light was no doubt the same – and just as rich.

Nature Notes

Dandelions

Incorrigible, brash,
They brightened the cinder path of my childhood,
Unsubtle, the opposite of primroses,
But, unlike primroses, capable
Of growing anywhere, railway track, pierhead,
Like our extrovert friends who never
Make us fall in love, yet fill
The primroseless roseless gaps.

Cats

Incorrigible, uncommitted,
They leavened the long flat hours of my childhood,
Subtle, the opposite of dogs,
And, unlike dogs, capable
Of flirting, falling, and yawning anywhere,
Like women who want no contract
But going their own way
Make the way of their lovers lighter.

Corncrakes

Incorrigible, unmusical,
They bridged the surrounding hedge of my childhood,
Unsubtle, the opposite of blackbirds,
But, unlike blackbirds, capable
Anywhere they are of endorsing summer
Like loud men around the corner
Whom we never see but whose raucous
Voices can give us confidence.

The Sea

Incorrigible, ruthless,
It rattled the shingly beach of my childhood,
Subtle, the opposite of earth,
And, unlike earth, capable
Any time at all of proclaiming eternity
Like something or someone to whom
We have to surrender, finding
Through that surrender life.

Sleeping Winds

North

The wind was curled in a ball asleep in a tree
With a young man cutting a heart on the bark;
Something came into the absence of mind of the wind,
He threw off the green and yawned himself over the sky;
The young man also grew to the height of a cloud
And was loud and rapid and free and never to die.

East

The wind was slumped on a charpoy in the bazaar,
Her breasts heavy with history; something crept
Slyly under her sari at dead of noon
And while the city slept she craved for water
And jumped to her feet and brushed the flies from her eyes
And took her pitcher and ran to the well of her own monsoon.

West

The wind lay still on the deck of Brandan's ship
While the sailors tried to rouse her; she never stirred
Till Brandan joined his hands and, coincidence or not,
She got on her knees and filled her lungs and put
Her lips to the sail and puffed. The long-lost ship
Flew home and into legend like a bird.

South

The wind had hidden his head in a pit in the sand
Of an uncrossable desert; something slid
Into his lack of ear, he gradually uncurled
Like a king cobra, rose and spread his hood
And swayed in time with what the charmer piped,
In time with Time, to wreck or bless the world.

Sunday in the Park

No sunlight ever. Bleak trees whisper ironies,
Carolina duck and Canada goose forget
Their world across the water, red geraniums
Enhance the chill, dark glasses mirror ironies,
The prams are big with doom, the walkers-out forget
Why they are out, London is lost, geraniums
Stick it out in the wind, old men feel lost
But stick it out and refugees forget
Pretences and grow sad while ironies
Frill out from sprinklers on the green veneer
That screens the tubes in which congested trains
Get stuck like enemas or ironies
Half lost between the lines while dachshunds run
Like centipedes and no one knows the time
Whatever foreigners ask it. Here is Sunday:
And on the seventh day He rested. The Tree
Forgets both good and evil in irony.

Variation on Heraclitus

Even the walls are flowing, even the ceiling,
Nor only in terms of physics; the pictures
Bob on each picture rail like floats on a line
While the books on the shelves keep reeling
Their titles out into space and the carpet
Keeps flying away to Arabia nor can this be where I stood –
Where I shot the rapids I mean – when I signed
On a line that rippled away with a pen that melted
Nor can this now be the chair – the chairoplane of a chair –
That I sat in the day that I thought I had made up my mind
And as for that standard lamp it too keeps waltzing away
Down an unbridgeable Ganges where nothing is standard
And lights are but lit to be drowned in honour and spite of some dark
And vanishing goddess. No, whatever you say,
Reappearance presumes disappearance, it may not be nice
Or proper or easily analysed not to be static
But none of your slide snide rules can catch what is sliding so fast
And, all you advisers on this by the time it is that,
I just do not want your advice
Nor need you be troubled to pin me down in my room
Since the room and I will escape for I tell you flat:
One cannot live in the same room twice.

Reflections

The mirror above my fireplace reflects the reflected
Room in my window; I look in the mirror at night
And see two rooms, the first where left is right
And the second, beyond the reflected window, corrected
But there I am standing back to my back. The standard
Lamp comes thrice in my mirror, twice in my window,
The fire in the mirror lies two rooms away through the window,
The fire in the window lies one room away down the terrace,
My actual room stands sandwiched between confections
Of night and lights and glass and in both directions
I can see beyond and through the reflections the street lamps
At home outdoors where my indoors rooms lie stranded,
Where a taxi perhaps will drive in through the bookcase
Whose books are not for reading and past the fire
Which gives no warmth and pull up by my desk
At which I cannot write since I am not lefthanded.

Hold-up

The lights were red, refused to change,
Ash-ends grew longer, no one spoke,
The papers faded in their hands,
The bubbles in the football pools
Went flat, the hot news froze, the dates
They could not keep were dropped like charred
Matches, the girls no longer flagged
Their sex, besides the code was lost,
The engine stalled, a tall glass box
On the pavement held a corpse in pickle
His ear still cocked, and no one spoke,
No number rang, for miles behind
The other buses nudged and blared
And no one dared get out. The conductress
Was dark and lost, refused to change.

The Wiper

Through purblind night the wiper
Reaps a swathe of water
On the screen; we shudder on
  And hardly hold the road,
All we can see a segment
Of blackly shining asphalt
With the wiper moving across it
  Clearing, blurring, clearing.

But what to say of the road?
The monotony of its hardly
Visible camber, the mystery
  Of its far invisible margins,
Will these be always with us,
The night being broken only
By lights that pass or meet us
  From others in moving boxes?

Boxes of glass and water,
Upholstered, equipped with dials
Professing to tell the distance
  We have gone, the speed we are going.
But never a gauge nor needle
To tell us where we are going
Or when day will come, supposing
  This road exists in daytime.

For now we cannot remember
Where we were when it was not
Night, when it was not raining,
  Before this car moved forward
And the wiper backward and forward
Lighting so little before us
Of a road that, crouching forward,
  We watch move always towards us,

Which through the tiny segment
Cleared and blurred by the wiper
Is sucked in under the axle
   To be spewed behind us and lost
While we, dazzled by darkness,
Haul the black future towards us
Peeling the skin from our hands;
   And yet we hold the road.

The Truisms

His father gave him a box of truisms
Shaped like a coffin, then his father died;
The truisms remained on the mantelpiece
As wooden as the playbox they had been packed in
Or that other his father skulked inside.

Then he left home, left the truisms behind him
Still on the mantelpiece, met love, met war,
Sordor, disappointment, defeat, betrayal,
Till through disbeliefs he arrived at a house
He could not remember seeing before,

And he walked straight in; it was where he had come from
And something told him the way to behave.
He raised his hand and blessed his home;
The truisms flew and perched on his shoulders
And a tall tree sprouted from his father's grave.

The Blasphemies

The sin against the Holy . . . though what
He wondered was it? Cold in his bed
He thought: If I think those words I know
Yet must not be thinking – Come to the hurdle
And I shall be damned through thinking Damn –
But Whom? But no! Those words are unthinkable;
Damn anyone else, but once I – No,
Here lies the unforgivable blasphemy.
So pulling the cold sheets over his head
He swore to himself he had not thought
Those words he knew but never admitted.
To be damned at seven years old was early.

Ten years later, his Who's Who
No longer cosmic, he turned to parody –
Prayers, hymns, the Apostles' Creed –
Preening himself as a gay blasphemer,
But what is a practical joke in a world
Of nonsense, what is a rational attitude
Towards politics in a world of ciphers,
Towards sex if you lack all lust, towards art
If you do not believe in communication?
And what is a joke about God if you do not
Accept His existence? Where is the blasphemy?
No Hell at seventeen feels empty.

Rising thirty, he had decided
God was a mere expletive, a cheap one,
No longer worth a laugh, no longer
A proper occasion to prove one's freedom
By denying something not worth denying.
So humanism was all and the only
Sin was the sin against the Human –
But you could not call it Ghost for that
Was merely emotive; the only – you could not
Call it sin for that was emotive –
The only failure was not to face
The facts. But at thirty what are the facts?

Ten years later, in need of myth,
He thought: I can use my childhood symbols
Divorced from their context, Manger and Cross
Could do very well for Tom Dick and Harry –
Have we not all of us been in a war
So have we not carried call it a cross
Which was never our fault? Yet how can a cross
Be never your fault? The words of the myth,
Now merely that and no longer faith,
Melt in his hands which were never proved
Hard as nails, nor can he longer
Speak for the world – or himself – at forty.

Forty to fifty. In ten years
He grew to feel the issue irrelevant:
Tom Dick and Harry were not Christ
And whether Christ were God or not
And whether there were a God or not
The word was inadequate. For himself
He was not Tom or Dick or Harry,
Let alone God, he was merely fifty,
No one and nowhere else, a walking
Question but no more cheap than any
Question or quest is cheap. The sin
Against the Holy Ghost – What is it?

Selva Oscura

A house can be haunted by those who were never there
If there was where they were missed. Returning to such
Is it worse if you miss the same or another or none?
The haunting anyway is too much.
You have to leave the house to clear the air.

A life can be haunted by what it never was
If that were merely glimpsed. Lost in the maze
That means yourself and never out of the wood
These days, though lost, will be all your days;
Life, if you leave it, must be left for good.

And yet for good can be also where I am,
Stumbling among dark tree-trunks, should I meet
One sudden shaft of light from the hidden sky
Or, finding bluebells bathe my feet,
Know that the world, though more, is also I.

Perhaps suddenly too I strike a clearing and see
Some unknown house – or was it mine? – but now
It welcomes whom I miss in welcoming me;
The door swings open and a hand
Beckons to all the life my days allow.

All Over Again

As if I had known you for years drink to me only if
Those frontiers have never changed on the mad map of the years
And all our tears were earned and this were the first cliff
From which we embraced the sea and these were the first words
We spread to lure the birds that nested in our day
As if it were always morning their dawnsong theirs and ours
And waking no one else me and you only now
Under the brow of a blue and imperturbable hill
Where still time stands and plays his bland and hemlock pipe
And the ripe moment tugs yet declines to fall and all
The years we had not met forget themselves in this
One kiss ingathered world and outward rippling bell
To the rim of the cup of the sky and leave it only there
Near into far blue into blue all over again
Notwithstanding unique all over all again
Of which to speak requires new fires of the tongue some trick
Of the light in the dark of the muted voice of the turning wild
World yet calm in her storm gay in her ancient rocks
To preserve today one kiss in this skybound timeless cup
Nor now shall I ask for anything more of future or past
This being last and first sound sight on eyes and ears
And each long then and there suspended on this cliff
Shining and slicing edge that reflects the sun as if
This one Between were All and we in love for years.

Soap Suds

This brand of soap has the same smell as once in the big
House he visited when he was eight: the walls of the bathroom open
To reveal a lawn where a great yellow ball rolls back through a hoop
To rest at the head of a mallet held in the hands of a child.

And these were the joys of that house: a tower with a telescope;
Two great faded globes, one of the earth, one of the stars;
A stuffed black dog in the hall; a walled garden with bees;
A rabbit warren; a rockery; a vine under glass; the sea.

To which he has now returned. The day of course is fine
And a grown-up voice cries Play! The mallet slowly swings,
Then crack, a great gong booms from the dog-dark hall and the ball
Skims forward through the hoop and then through the next and then

Through hoops where no hoops were and each dissolves in turn
And the grass has grown head-high and an angry voice cries Play!
But the ball is lost and the mallet slipped long since from the hands
Under the running tap that are not the hands of a child.

Déjà Vu

It does not come round in hundreds of thousands of years,
It comes round in the split of a wink, you will be sitting exactly
Where you are now and scratching your elbow, the train
Will be passing exactly as now and saying It does not come round,
It does not come round, It does not come round, and compactly
The wheels will mark time on the rails and the bird in the air
Sit tight in its box and the same bean of coffee be ground
That is now in the mill and I know what you're going to say
For all this has happened before, we both have been through the mill,
Through our Magnus Annus, and now could all but call it a day
Were it not that scratching your elbow you are too lovely by half
So that, whatever the rules we might be supposed to obey,
Our love must extend beyond time because time is itself in arrears
So this double vision must pass and past and future unite
And where we were told to kowtow we can snap our fingers and
laugh
And now, as you watch, I will take this selfsame pencil and write:
It does not come round in hundreds of thousands of years.

Round the Corner

Round the corner was always the sea. Our childhood
Tipping the sand from its shoes on return from holiday
Knew there was more where it came from, as there was more
Seaweed to pop and horizon to blink at. Later
Our calf loves yearned for union in solitude somewhere
Round that corner where Xenophon crusted with parasangs
Knew he was home, where Columbus feared he was not,
And the Bible said there would be no more of it. Round
That corner regardless there will be always a realm
Undercutting its banks with repeated pittance of spray,
The only anarchic democracy, where we are all vicarious
Citizens; which we remember as we remember a person
Whose wrists are springs to spring a trap or rock
A cradle; whom we remember when the sand falls out on the carpet
Or the exiled shell complains or a wind from round the corner
Carries the smell of wrack or the taste of salt, or a wave
Touched to steel by the moon twists a gimlet in memory.
Round the corner is – sooner or later – the sea.

The Suicide

And this, ladies and gentlemen, whom I am not in fact
Conducting, was his office all those minutes ago,
This man you never heard of. There are the bills
In the intray, the ash in the ashtray, the grey memoranda stacked
Against him, the serried ranks of the box-files, the packed
Jury of his unanswered correspondence
Nodding under the paperweight in the breeze
From the window by which he left; and here is the cracked
Receiver that never got mended and here is the jotter
With his last doodle which might be his own digestive tract
Ulcer and all or might be the flowery maze
Through which he had wandered deliciously till he stumbled
Suddenly finally conscious of all he lacked
On a manhole under the hollyhocks. The pencil
Point had obviously broken, yet, when he left this room
By catdrop sleight-of-foot or simple vanishing act,
To those who knew him for all that mess in the street
This man with the shy smile has left behind
Something that was intact.

Flower Show

Marooned by night in a canvas cathedral under bare bulbs
He plods the endless aisles not daring to close an eye
To massed brass bands of flowers; these flowers are not to pluck
Which (cream cheese, paper, glass, all manner of textile and plastic)
Having long since forgotten, if they ever knew, the sky
Are grown, being forced, uprooted.

Squidlike, phallic or vulvar, hypnotic, idiotic, oleaginous,
Fanged or whaleboned, wattled or balding, brimstone or cold
As trout or seaweed, these blooms, ogling or baneful, all
Keep him in their blind sights; he tries to stare them down
But they are too many, too unreal, their aims are one, the controlled
Aim of a firing party.

So bandage his eyes since he paid to come in but somehow forgot
To follow the others out – and now there is no way out
Except that his inturned eyes before he falls may show him
Some nettled orchard, tousled hedge, some garden even
Where flowers, whether they boast or insinuate, whisper or shout,
Still speak a living language.

The Taxis

In the first taxi he was alone tra-la,
No extras on the clock. He tipped ninepence
But the cabby, while he thanked him, looked askance
As though to suggest someone had bummed a ride.

In the second taxi he was alone tra-la
But the clock showed sixpence extra; he tipped according
And the cabby from out his muffler said: 'Make sure
You have left nothing behind tra-la between you.'

In the third taxi he was alone tra-la
But the tip-up seats were down and there was an extra
Charge of one-and-sixpence and an odd
Scent that reminded him of a trip to Cannes.

As for the fourth taxi, he was alone
Tra-la when he hailed it but the cabby looked
Through him and said: 'I can't tra-la well take
So many people, not to speak of the dog.'

After the Crash

When he came to he knew
Time must have passed because
The asphalt was high with hemlock
Through which he crawled to his crash
Helmet and found it no more
Than his wrinkled hand what it was.

Yet life seemed still going on:
He could hear the signals bounce
Back from the moon and the hens
Fire themselves black in the batteries
And the silence of small blind cats
Debating whether to pounce.

Then he looked up and marked
The gigantic scales in the sky,
The pan on the left dead empty
And the pan on the right dead empty,
And knew in the dead, dead calm
It was too late to die.

Another Cold May

With heads like chessmen, bishop or queen,
The tulips tug at their roots and mourn
In inaudible frequencies, the move
Is the wind's, not theirs; fender to fender
The cars will never emerge, not even
Should their owners emerge to claim them, the move
Is time's, not theirs; elbow to elbow
Inside the roadhouse drinks are raised
And downed, and downed, the pawns and drains
Are blocked, are choked, the move is nil,
The lounge is, like the carpark, full,
The tulips also feel the chill
And tilting leeward do no more
Than mimic a bishop's move, the square
Ahead remains ahead, their petals
Will merely fall and choke the drains
Which will be all; this month remains
False animation of failed levitation,
The move is time's, the loss is ours.

Ravenna

What do I remember of my visit to Ravenna? Firstly,
That I had come from Venice where I had come from Greece
So that my eyes seemed dim and the world flat. Secondly,
That after Tintoretto's illusory depth and light
The mosaics knocked me flat. There they stood. The geese
Had hissed as they pecked the corn from Theodora's groin,
Yet here she stands on the wall of San Vitale, as bright
As life and a long shot taller, self-made empress,
Who patronised the monophysites and the Greens
And could have people impaled. There was also and thirdly the long-
Lost naval port of Caesar, surviving now in the name
In Classe: the sea today is behind the scenes
Like his Liburnian galleys. What went wrong
With Byzantium as with Rome went slowly, their fame
Sunk in malarial marsh. The flat lands now
Are ruled by a sugar refinery and a church,
Sant' Apollinare in Classe. What do I remember of Ravenna?
A bad smell mixed with glory, and the cold
Eyes that belie the tessellated gold.

Charon

The conductor's hands were black with money;
Hold on to your ticket, he said, the inspector's
Mind is black with suspicion, and hold on to
That dissolving map. We moved through London,
We could see the pigeons through the glass but failed
To hear their rumours of wars, we could see
The lost dog barking but never knew
That his bark was as shrill as a cock crowing,
We just jogged on, at each request
Stop there was a crowd of aggressively vacant
Faces, we just jogged on, eternity
Gave itself airs in revolving lights
And then we came to the Thames and all
The bridges were down, the further shore
Was lost in fog, so we asked the conductor
What we should do. He said: Take the ferry
Faute de mieux. We flicked the flashlight
And there was the ferryman just as Virgil
And Dante had seen him. He looked at us coldly
And his eyes were dead and his hands on the oar
Were black with obols and varicose veins
Marbled his calves and he said to us coldly:
If you want to die you will have to pay for it.

The Introduction

They were introduced in a grave glade
And she frightened him because she was young
And thus too late. Crawly crawly
Went the twigs above their heads and beneath
The grass beneath their feet the larvae
Split themselves laughing. Crawly crawly
Went the cloud above the treetops reaching
For a sun that lacked the nerve to set
And he frightened her because he was old
And thus too early. Crawly crawly
Went the string quartet that was tuning up
In the back of the mind. You two should have met
Long since, he said, or else not now.
The string quartet in the back of the mind
Was all tuned up with nowhere to go.
They were introduced in a green grave.

Birthright

When I was born the row began,
I had never asked to be a man;
They never asked if I could ride
But shouted at me 'Come outside!',
Then hauled the rearing beast along
And said: 'Your charger, right or wrong.'
His ears went back and so did I,
I said 'To mount him means to die',
They said 'Of course'; the nightmare neighed
And I felt foolish and afraid.
The sun came up, my feet stuck fast,
The minutes, hours, and years went past,
More chances missed than I could count,
The stable boys cried: 'Time to mount!'
My jaw dropped and I gaped from drouth:
My gift horse looked me in the mouth.

Sports Page

Nostalgia, incantation, escape,
Courts and fields of the Ever Young:
On your Marks! En Garde! Scrum Down! Over!
On the ropes, on the ice, breasting the tape,
Our Doppelgänger is bounced and flung
While the ball squats in the air like a spider
Threading the horizon round the goalposts
And we, though never there, give tongue.

Yet our Doppelgänger rides once more
Over the five-barred gates and flames
In metaphors filched from magic and music
With a new witch broom and a rattling score
And the names we read seem more than names,
Potions or amulets, till we remember
The lines of print are always sidelines
And all our games funeral games.

The Habits

When they put him in rompers the habits
Fanned out to close in, they were dressed
In primary colours and each of them
Carried a rattle and a hypodermic;
His parents said it was all for the best.

Next, the barracks of boys: the habits
Slapped him on the back, they were dressed
In pinstripe trousers and carried
A cheque book, a passport, and a sjambok;
The master said it was all for the best.

And then came the women: the habits
Pretended to leave, they were dressed
In bittersweet undertones and carried
A Parthian shaft and an affidavit;
The adgirl said it was all for the best.

Age became middle: the habits
Made themselves at home, they were dressed
In quilted dressing-gowns and carried
A decanter, a siphon, and a tranquillizer;
The computer said it was all for the best.

Then age became real: the habits
Outstayed their welcome, they were dressed
In nothing and carried nothing.
He said: If you won't go, I go.
The Lord God said it was all for the best.

from As in their Time

(i)

They were so mean they could not between them
Leave one tip behind them; the others
Tipped so wildly it made no sense,
When the cold computer gathered the leavings
It broke about even, made no sense.

(ii)

Polyglot, albeit illiterate,
He stood on a crumbling tower of Babel
Cured of heredity, and though
His idol had a brain of clay
He could not read the cuneiform.

(vi)

He had clowned it through. Being born
For either the heights or the depths
He had bowled his hoop on the level
Arena; the hoop was a wheel
Of fire but he clowned it through.

He was to be found in directories,
Admiring asides and footnotes,
Flowers by request. When he entered
A room it at once was a morgue
To tip people off he had entered.

(x)

Citizen of an ever-expanding
Universe, burning smokeless fuel,
He had lived among plastic gear so long
When they decided to fingerprint him
He left no fingerprints at all.

(xii)

As a child showed promise. No need to push him,
Everyone said. Then came the drought
And after that, on his twenty-first birthday,
A cloud no bigger than a god's hand
And after that there was no need to push him.

Star-gazer

Forty-two years ago (to me if to no one else
The number is of some interest) it was a brilliant starry night
And the westward train was empty and had no corridors
So darting from side to side I could catch the unwonted sight
Of those almost intolerably bright
Holes, punched in the sky, which excited me partly because
Of their Latin names and partly because I had read in the textbooks
How very far off they were, it seemed their light
Had left them (some at least) long years before I was.

And this remembering now I mark that what
Light was leaving some of them at least then,
Forty-two years ago, will never arrive
In time for me to catch it, which light when
It does get here may find that there is not
Anyone left alive
To run from side to side in a late night train
Admiring it and adding noughts in vain.

Coda

Maybe we knew each other better
When the night was young and unrepeated
And the moon stood still over Jericho.

So much for the past; in the present
There are moments caught between heart-beats
When maybe we know each other better.

But what is that clinking in the darkness?
Maybe we shall know each other better
When the tunnels meet beneath the mountain.

Index of Titles